SPECTRUM

Phonics

Grade 2

Spectrum

An imprint of Carson-Dellosa Publishing LLC
Greensboro, North Carolina

Spectrum
An imprint of Carson-Dellosa Publishing LLC
P.O. Box 35665
Greensboro, NC 27425 USA

06-166111151

Table of Contents

Index of Skills

Phonics Grade 2

Numerals indicate the exercise pages on which these skills appear.

Auditory Skills

Associate sounds with letters—all activities

Discriminate consonant sounds—40, 41, 42, 43, 44, 45, 46, 47, 48, 49, 50, 51, 52, 53, 54, 55, 56, 57, 58, 59, 60, 61, 62, 63, 64, 65, 66, 67, 68, 69, 70, 71, 72, 73, 74, 75, 76, 99, 100, 101, 102, 103, 104

Discriminate initial sounds—6, 7, 46, 47, 48, 49, 50, 51, 52, 62, 63, 64, 65, 66, 67, 68, 69, 99, 100, 103, 104

Discriminate final sounds—6, 7, 53, 54, 55, 56, 57, 58, 59, 60, 61, 66, 101, 102, 103, 104

Discriminate vowel sounds—8, 9, 10, 11, 12, 13, 14, 15, 16, 17, 18, 19, 20, 21, 22, 23, 24, 25, 26, 27, 28, 29, 30, 31, 32, 33, 34, 35, 36, 37, 38, 39, 77, 78, 79, 80, 81, 82, 83, 84, 85, 86, 87, 88, 89, 90, 91, 92, 93, 94, 95, 96, 97, 98, 105, 106, 107, 108, 109, 110, 111, 112, 113, 114, 115, 116, 117, 118, 119, 120, 121

Following directions—all activities

Recognize rhyming words—12, 16, 18, 21, 31, 33, 53, 56, 59, 77, 87, 89, 102, 110, 120

Visual Skills

Discriminate pictures/identify objects—6, 7, 8, 9, 11, 12, 13, 14, 15, 16, 17, 18, 19, 20, 21, 22, 24, 25, 26, 27, 28, 29, 30, 31, 32, 33, 34, 35, 36, 37, 38, 40, 41, 42, 43, 44, 45, 46, 47, 48, 49, 50, 51, 52, 53, 54, 55, 56, 57, 58, 59, 60, 61, 62, 63, 65, 66, 67, 68, 70, 71, 73, 75, 76, 77, 78, 80, 81, 83, 84, 86, 87, 88, 89, 90, 92, 94, 95, 96, 98, 99, 100, 101, 102, 103, 105, 106, 107, 108, 109, 110, 112, 114, 115, 117, 118, 120, 121

Discriminate words—9, 10, 11, 12, 13, 14, 15, 16, 17, 18, 19, 20, 21, 22, 23, 24, 26, 27, 28, 29, 30, 31, 32, 33, 34, 35, 39, 40, 41, 42, 43, 45, 47, 49, 51, 52, 53, 55, 56, 57, 58, 59, 60, 61, 63, 64, 65, 68, 69, 70, 72, 73, 74, 76, 77, 78, 79, 80, 82, 83, 84, 85, 87, 88, 89, 90, 91, 92, 93, 94, 95, 96, 97, 100, 102, 103, 104, 105, 107, 109, 110, 111, 112, 113, 114, 116, 117, 119

Writing Skills

Write letters—6, 7, 23, 25, 27, 29, 31, 33, 37, 44, 46, 48, 50, 53, 56, 59, 62, 66, 67, 86, 99, 101, 106, 108, 115, 118

Write words—9, 10, 11, 12, 13, 14, 15, 16, 17, 18, 19, 20, 21, 22, 24, 25, 26, 27, 28, 29, 30, 31, 32, 33, 34, 35, 36, 38, 39, 40, 41, 42, 43, 45, 47, 49, 51, 52, 53, 55, 56, 58, 59, 61, 62, 64, 65, 68, 69, 70, 72, 73, 74, 76, 77, 78, 79, 80, 82, 83, 85, 86, 87, 88, 89, 90, 91, 92, 93, 94, 95, 96, 97, 98, 99, 100, 101, 102, 103, 104, 105, 106, 107, 108, 109, 110, 111, 112, 114, 115, 116, 117, 118, 119, 120, 121

Write sentences—13, 15, 19, 26, 47, 49, 51, 60, 63, 67, 68, 71, 73, 75, 80, 81, 83, 84, 92, 109, 113, 114

Short Vowels

a—8, 9, 10, 23, 24, 35, 36, 37, 38
e—11, 12, 13, 23, 24, 35, 36, 37, 38, 81, 82, 86, 98
i—14, 15, 16, 23, 24, 35, 36, 37, 38
o—17, 18, 19, 23, 24, 35, 36, 37, 38
u—20, 21, 22, 23, 24, 35, 36, 37, 38

Long Vowels

a—25, 26, 33, 34, 35, 36, 37, 38, 77, 78, 79, 86, 98
e—80, 81, 82, 86, 95, 96, 97, 98
i—27, 28, 33, 34, 35, 36, 37, 38
o—29, 30, 33, 34, 35, 36, 37, 38, 83, 84, 85, 86
u—31, 32, 33, 34, 35, 36, 37, 38
y—95, 96, 97, 98

Other Vowel Sounds

ar—105, 106, 110, 111, 112, 113
au—89, 90, 91, 94
aw—89, 90, 91, 94
er—105, 106 , 111, 112
ew—92, 93, 94
ir—107, 108, 110, 111, 112, 113
oi—114, 115, 116, 120, 121
oo—87, 88, 94, 98
or—107, 108, 110, 111, 112, 113
ou—117, 118, 119, 120, 121
ow—117, 118, 119, 120, 121
oy—114, 115, 116, 120, 121
ur—109, 110, 111, 112, 113

Consonant Blends—46, 47, 48, 49, 50, 51, 52, 53, 54, 55, 56, 57, 58, 59, 60, 61, 62, 63, 64, 65, 66, 102, 103, 104

Consonant Pairs—99, 100, 101, 102, 103, 104

Silent Consonants—67, 68, 69, 70, 71, 72, 73, 74, 75, 76

Review: Beginning and Ending Sounds

Directions: Say the name of each picture. Write the missing letter or letters to complete each word.

ta___

___an

___u___

___op

si___

___u___

___eb

___a___

Name _____

Review: Beginning and Ending Sounds

Directions: Say the name of each picture. Write the missing letter or letters to complete each word.

___an

___a___

do___

___i___

___op

be___

___a___

___a___

Name _____

Short a

Directions: Connect all the pictures whose names have the short **a** sound from the cat to the bag.

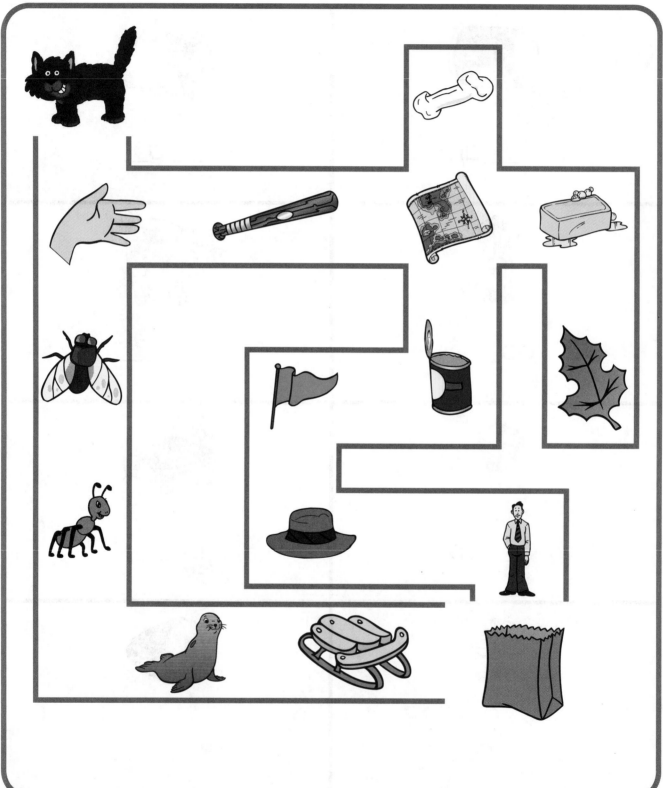

Short a

Directions: Write the word from the Word Box that names each picture.

van	cab	cap	apple	map	pan
add	ham	ant	can	hand	ax

Short a

Directions: Write the word from the Word Box that best completes each sentence.

| pan | hand | hat | has | ant | as | ham | apple | am |

1. An _____ is very tiny.

2. Can you _____ Dad the bag?

3. I wear a _____.

4. I _____ glad.

5. He is _____ tall as a yardstick.

6. Mom will fry fish in a _____.

7. We had _____ for lunch.

8. She _____ a new hat.

9. The _____ is red.

Name _____

Short e

Directions: Write the word from the Word Box that names each picture.

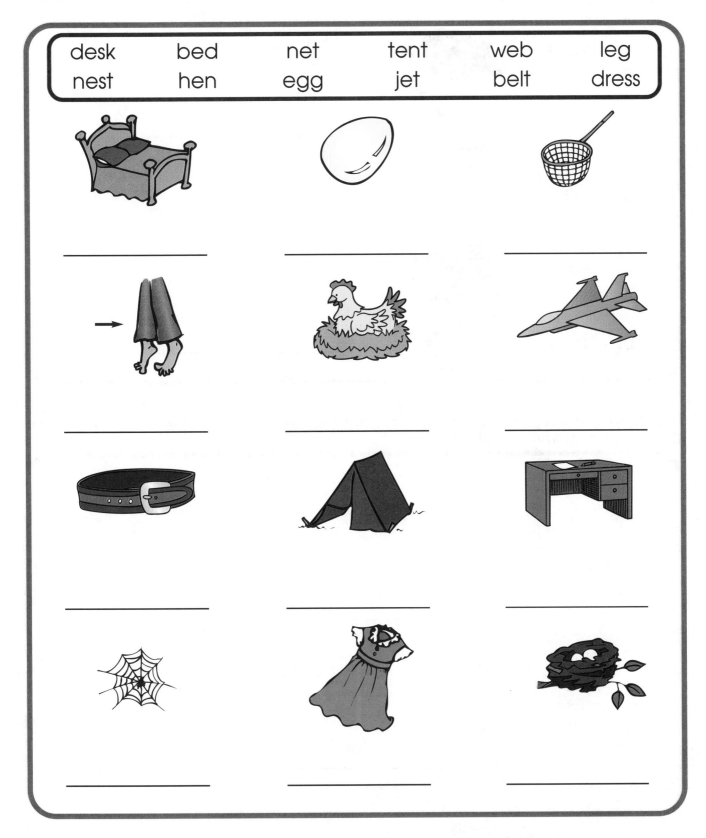

desk	bed	net	tent	web	leg
nest	hen	egg	jet	belt	dress

Short e

Directions: Write a word that rhymes with each word below.

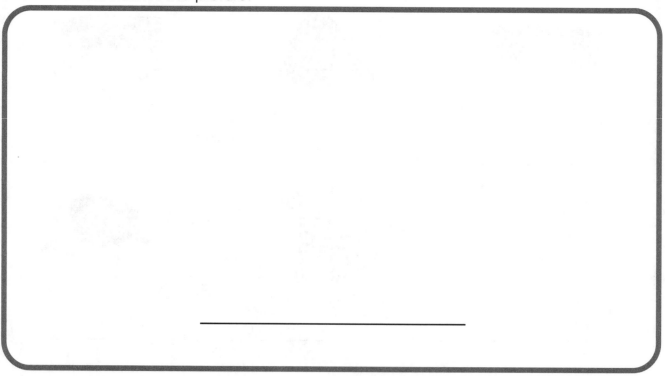

1. nest _____

2. net _____

3. jet _____

4. sled _____

5. hen _____

Directions: Draw a picture of something whose name has the short **e** sound. Then, write the word that names the picture.

_____

Short e

Directions: Write the word from the Word Box that best completes each sentence.

beg	smell	net	wet	nest

1. Dad had the frog in a _____.

2. The bird sleeps in its _____.

3. Can you _____ the flower?

4. The shirt is _____.

5. My dog likes to _____.

Directions: Write two short **e** words of your own. Then, use each word in a sentence.

1. _____   2. _____

1. _____

   _____

2. _____

   _____

Short i

Directions: Write the word from the Word Box that names each picture.

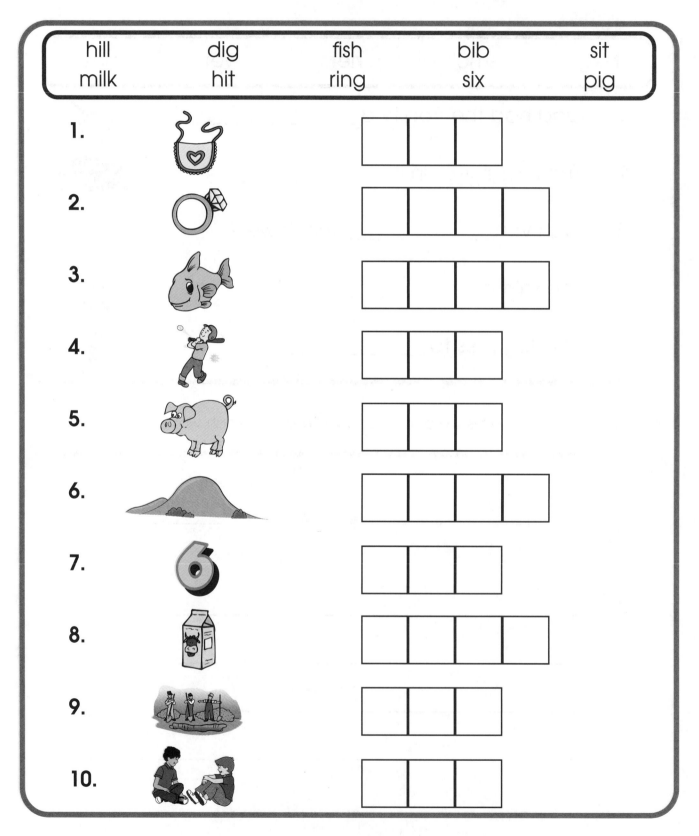

| hill | dig | fish | bib | sit |
| milk | hit | ring | six | pig |

1.

2.

3.

4.

5.

6.

7.

8.

9.

10.

Short i

Directions: Write the word from the Word Box that best completes each sentence.

| lid | zip | dig | milk | crib |

1. Spike likes to _____ in the yard.

2. Mom put the baby in the _____.

3. We drink _____ at lunch.

4. Tammy put the _____ on the pan.

5. I can _____ my coat.

Directions: Draw a picture of something whose name has the short **i** sound. Then, write a sentence that tells about your picture.

_____

_____

Short i

Directions: Draw a picture of something that rhymes with each word below. Then, write the rhyming word.

pig

_____

bib

_____

grill

_____

fish

_____

hit

_____

Short o

Directions: Write the word from the Word Box that names each picture.

dots	cot	lock	cob	box	doll
rod	top	pot	hop	fox	mop

Short o

Directions: Draw a picture of something that rhymes with each word below. Then, write the rhyming word.

box _____

mop _____

lock _____

spot _____

frog _____

Short o

Directions: Write the word from the Word Box that best completes each sentence.

hop	top	cot	hot	chop

1. Molly sleeps on the _____.

2. Dad can _____ with the ax.

3. The pot is very _____.

4. The bunny likes to _____.

5. Can you spin a _____?

Directions: Draw a picture of something whose name has the short **o** sound. Then, write a sentence that tells about your picture.

_____

_____

Short u

Directions: Write the word from the Word Box that names each picture.

| run | cub | pup | tub | nut | sun |
| bus | mug | hug | bug | bun | rug |

Short u

Directions: Draw a picture of something that rhymes with each word below. Then, write the rhyming word.

bun _____

jump _____

hug _____

cub _____

pup _____

Short u

Directions: Write the word from the Word Box that best completes each sentence.

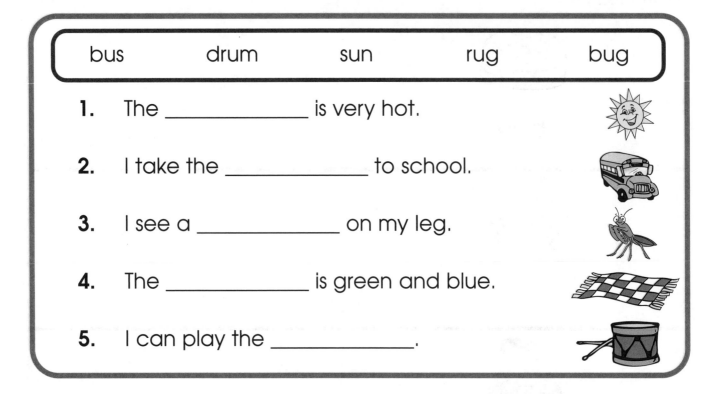

| bus | drum | sun | rug | bug |

1. The _____ is very hot.

2. I take the _____ to school.

3. I see a _____ on my leg.

4. The _____ is green and blue.

5. I can play the _____.

Directions: Draw a picture of something whose name has the short **u** sound. Then, write the word that names the picture.

_____

Name _____

Review: Short Vowels

Directions: Write a vowel in the middle of each puzzle that will make a word across and down.

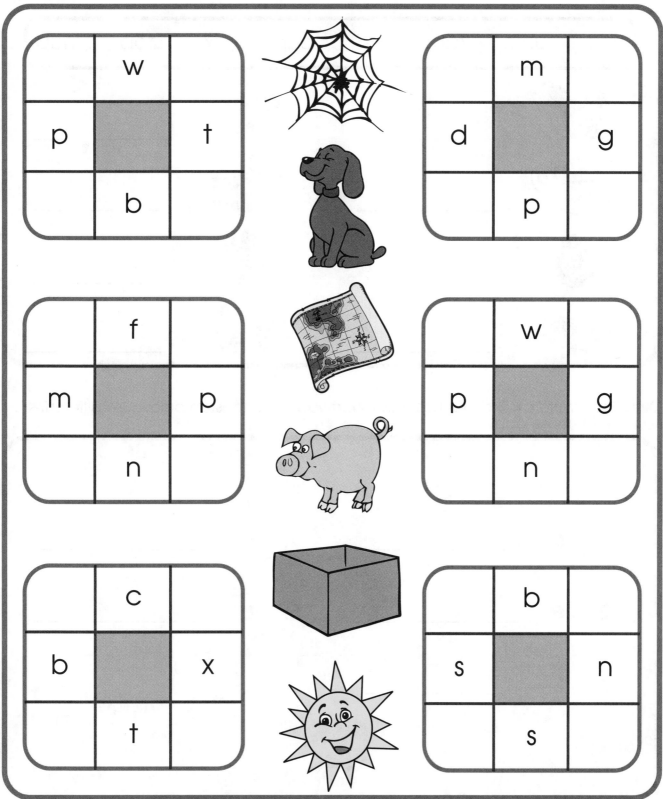

Check Up: Short Vowels

Directions: Write the word from the Word Box that names each picture.

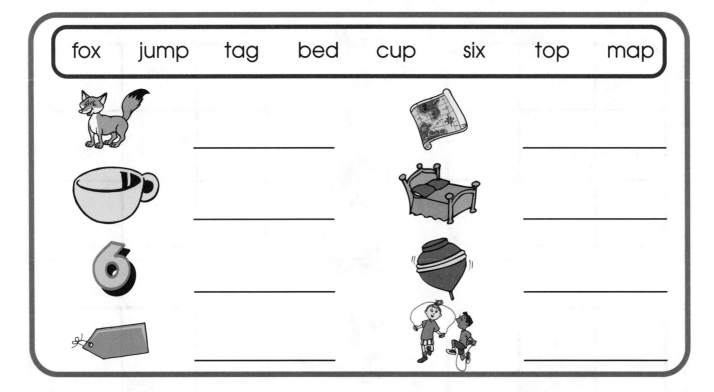

fox   jump   tag   bed   cup   six   top   map

_____

_____

_____

_____

_____

_____

Directions: Write a word that has each short vowel sound listed below. Use different words than those above.

1. **a** _____

2. **e** _____

3. **i** _____

4. **o** _____

5. **u** _____

Long a

Directions: Circle each picture that has the long **a** sound.

Directions: Fill in the missing letters **a** and **e** for each word. Then, write each word again.

1. r___k___ _____

2. c___p___ _____

3. s___f___ _____

4. v___s___ _____

5. c___n___ _____

Long a

Directions: Draw a picture of something that has the long **a** sound. Then, write a sentence that tells about your picture.

_____

_____

Directions: Write the word from the Word Box that best completes each sentence.

ape	lake	cane	vase	bake	game

1. We swim in the _____.

2. Mom put flowers in the _____.

3. Sam plays a _____.

4. I will _____ a cake.

5. Grandpa needs a _____ to walk.

6. We saw an _____ at the zoo.

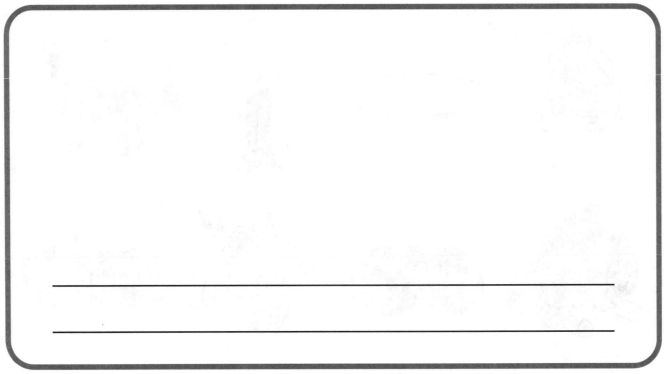

Long i

Directions: Draw a line to match each picture with its name.

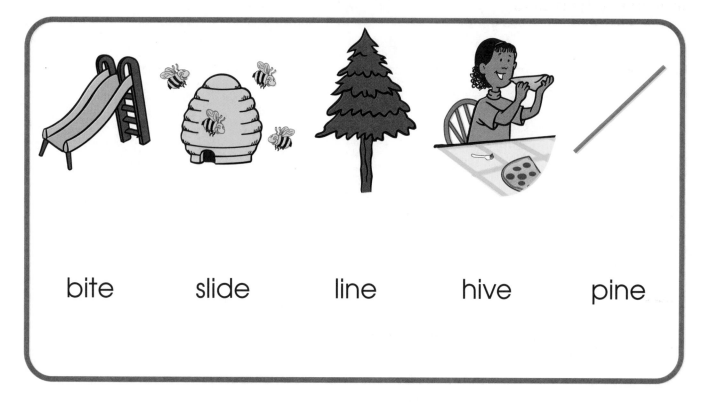

bite   slide   line   hive   pine

Directions: Write the missing letters **i** and **e** for each word. Then, write each word again.

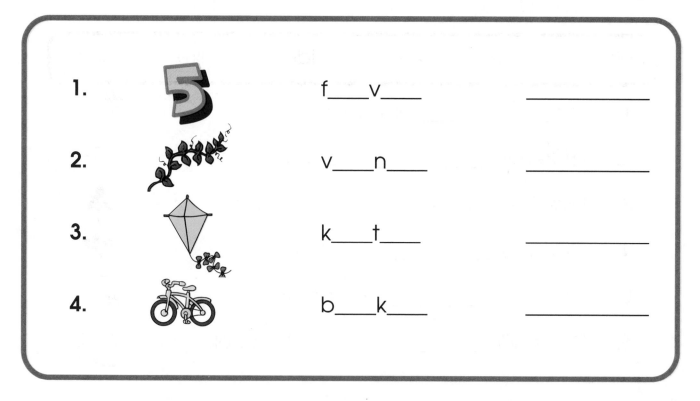

1. f___v___   _____

2. v___n___   _____

3. k___t___   _____

4. b___k___   _____

Name _____

Long i

Directions: Draw a picture of something that has the long **i** sound. Then, write the word that names the picture.

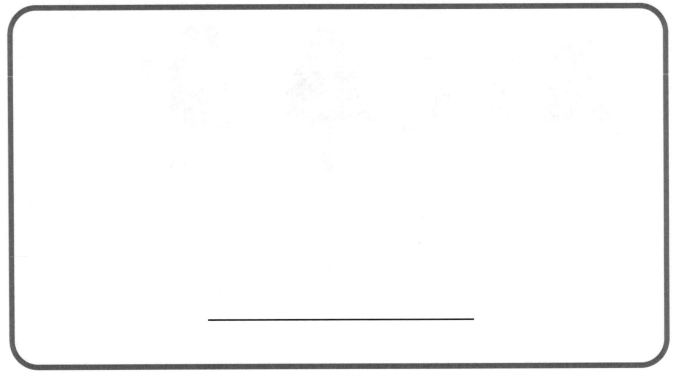

_____

Directions: Write the word from the Word Box that best completes each sentence.

bite	dive	kite	ride	bike	pine

1. My _____ is up in the tree.

2. I ride my _____ to school.

3. I like the smell of _____ trees.

4. Can you _____ a horse?

5. Take a _____ of the apple.

6. Dave will _____ into the pool.

Long o

Directions: Write the word from the Word Box that names each picture.

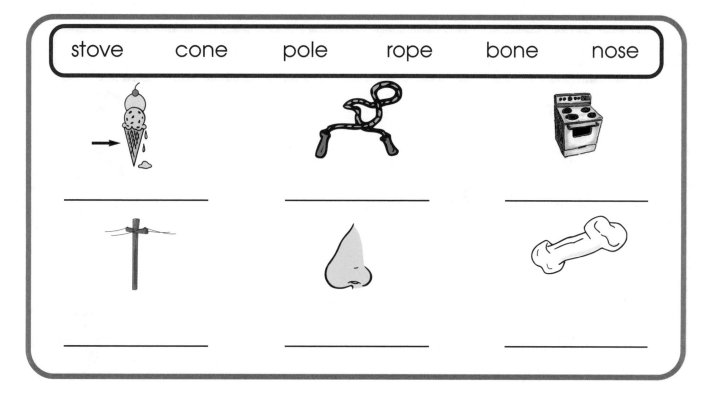

| stove | cone | pole | rope | bone | nose |

_____   _____   _____

_____   _____   _____

Directions: Write the missing letters **o** and **e** for each word. Then, write each word again.

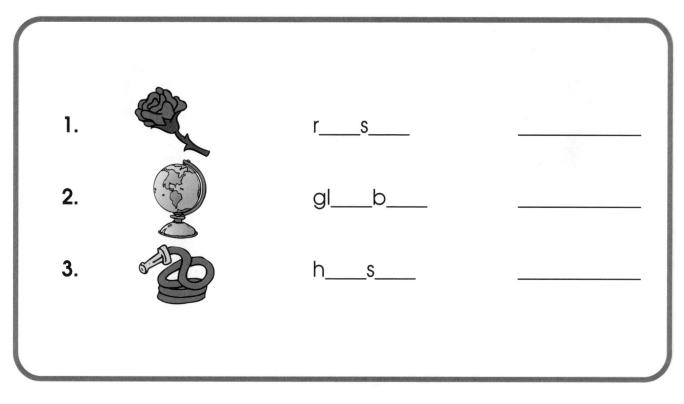

1.   r___s___   _____

2.   gl___b___   _____

3.   h___s___   _____

Long o

Directions: Write the word from the Word Box that best completes each sentence.

hose	note	rose	stove	rope	bone

1. Mom gave Dad a _____.

2. Put the _____ in the car.

3. Spike will give Fido a _____.

4. Can you sing that _____?

5. Dad has a green _____ in the yard.

6. The _____ is very hot.

Directions: Write the word that names each picture below.

_____   _____   _____

Long u

Directions: Write the missing letters **u** and **e** for each word. Then, write each word again.

1. t___n___   _____

2. m___l___   _____

3. d___n___   _____

4. c___t___   _____

5. c___b___   _____

Directions: Write a word that rhymes with each word below.

1. tube   _____

2. prune   _____

3. flute   _____

Long u

Directions: Circle the word that names the picture. Then, write the word on the line.

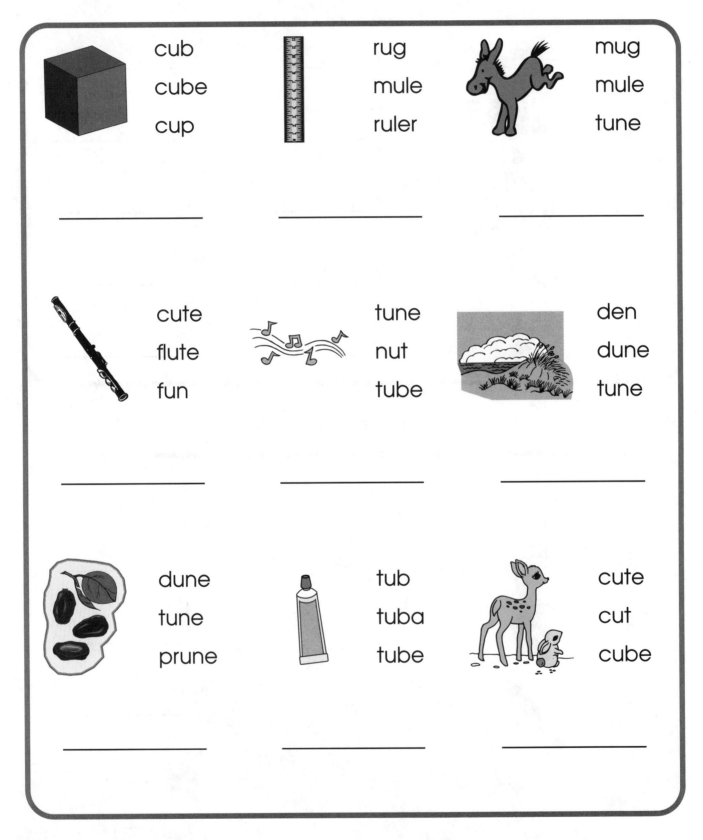

cub
cube
cup

_____

rug
mule
ruler

_____

mug
mule
tune

_____

cute
flute
fun

_____

tune
nut
tube

_____

den
dune
tune

_____

dune
tune
prune

_____

tub
tuba
tube

_____

cute
cut
cube

_____

Review: Long Vowels

Directions: Write the missing vowels to complete each word.

1. r___k___

2. r___b___

3. t___p___

4. t___b___

5. k___t___

Directions: Write a word that rhymes with each word below.

1. vine _____ 5. wave _____

2. gate _____ 6. like _____

3. hose _____ 7. tune _____

4. cube _____ 8. game _____

Check Up: Long Vowels

Directions: Write the word from the Word Box that names each picture.

| cape | safe | bike | vase | mule | bone |
| tube | prune | hose | cone | cube | nine |

Short and Long Vowels

Directions: Write the word from the Word Box that names each picture.

duck   pan   rod   skates   lips   tape
cub   dress   slide   cone   vine   flute

Short and Long Vowels

Directions: Write each picture name in the correct column.

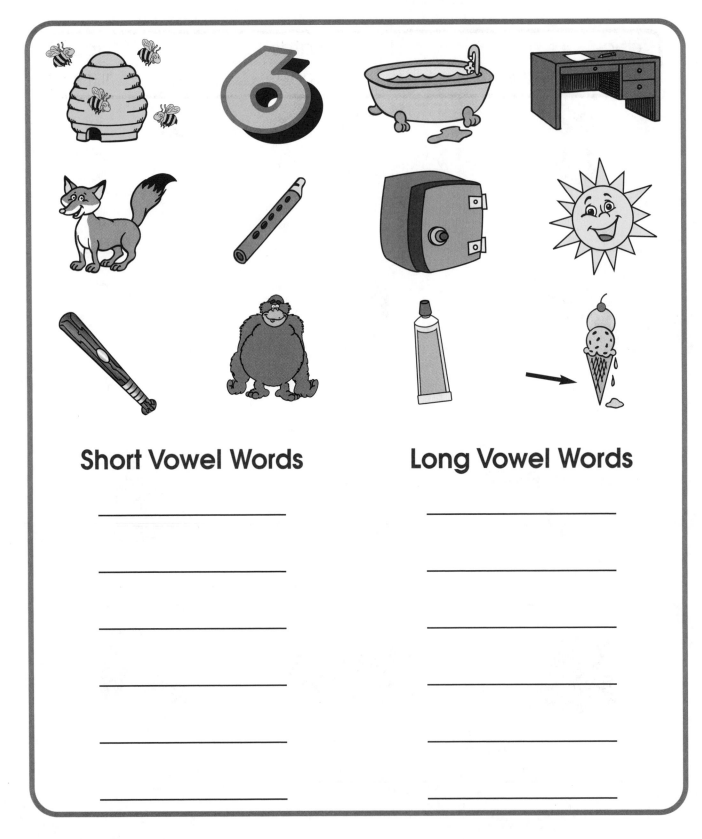

Short Vowel Words

_____

_____

_____

_____

_____

Long Vowel Words

_____

_____

_____

_____

_____

Short and Long Vowels

Directions: Write the missing vowel or vowels for each word.

1. b___g

2. b___k___

3. r___p___

4. b___d

5. n___s___

6. t___p

7. m___p

8. m___l___

9. b___b

10. p___n___

Short and Long Vowels

Directions: Draw a picture of something whose name has the vowel sound written in each box. Then, write the word that names each picture.

Long u	Short a	Short e
_____	_____	_____

Long i	Long o	Short i
_____	_____	_____

Short u	Long a	Short o
_____	_____	_____

Check Up: Short and Long Vowels

Directions: Circle the word that best completes each sentence. Then, write the word in the blank.

1. Lisa put the hat in the _____.

   bone   box   robe

2. A _____ is a very large animal.

   hag   hose   hog

3. The mother bear takes care of her _____.

   cube   cup   cub

4. Let's play a _____.

   gum   gate   game

5. I will play a _____ on the flute.

   tub   tube   tune

6. Put the _____ on the boat.

   robe   rope   nine

7. I like to go down the _____.

   five   fish   slide

8. He will wash the dog in the _____.

   tub   tube   tag

Hard and Soft c

Directions: The letter **c** can have the hard sound of **k**. It can also have the soft sound of **s**. Draw a line to match each word with its picture.

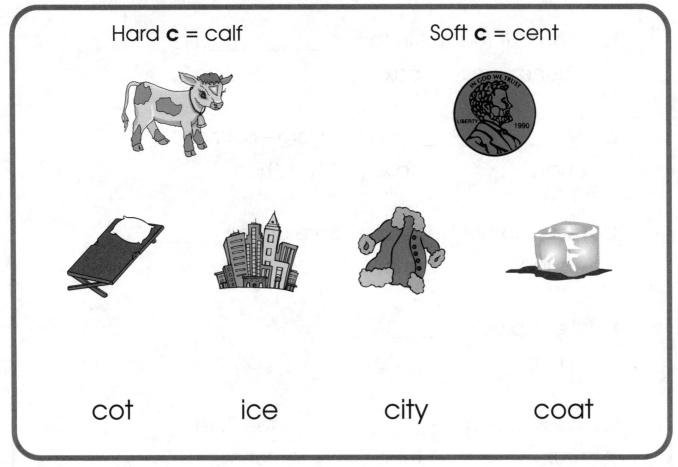

Hard **c** = calf   Soft **c** = cent

cot   ice   city   coat

Directions: Write each picture name from above in the correct column.

Hard c Words	Soft c Words
_____	_____
_____	_____

Hard and Soft c

Directions: Write the word from the Word Box that names each picture.

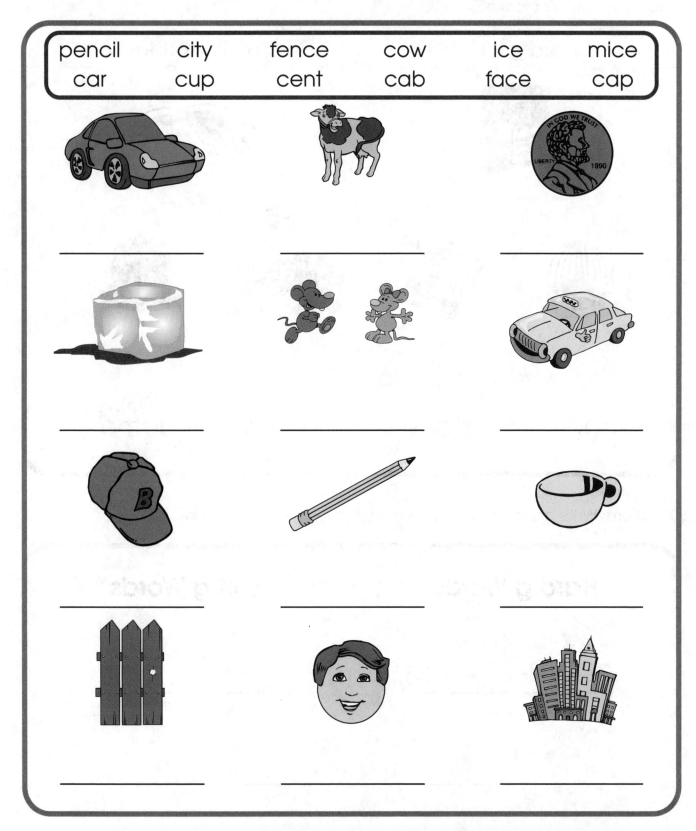

pencil	city	fence	cow	ice	mice
car	cup	cent	cab	face	cap

_____   _____   _____

_____   _____   _____

_____   _____   _____

_____   _____   _____

Hard and Soft g

Directions: The letter **g** can have a hard sound and a soft sound. Draw a line to match each word with its picture.

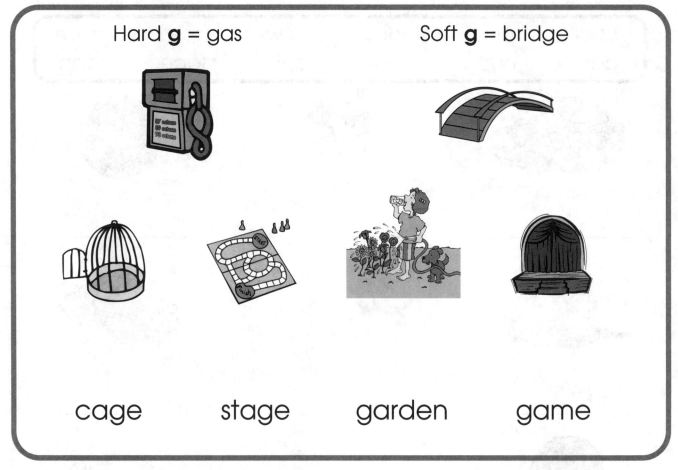

Hard **g** = gas   Soft **g** = bridge

cage   stage   garden   game

Directions: Write each picture name from above in the correct column.

Hard g Words	**Soft g Words**
_____	_____
_____	_____

Hard and Soft g

Directions: Write the word from the Word Box that names each picture.

wig	edge	judge	goat	gate	cage
stage	globe	dog	page	bridge	pig

Name _____

Review: Hard and Soft c and g

Directions: Write the missing letter **c** or **g** for each word. Then, circle the word *hard* or *soft* to tell how the letter sounds.

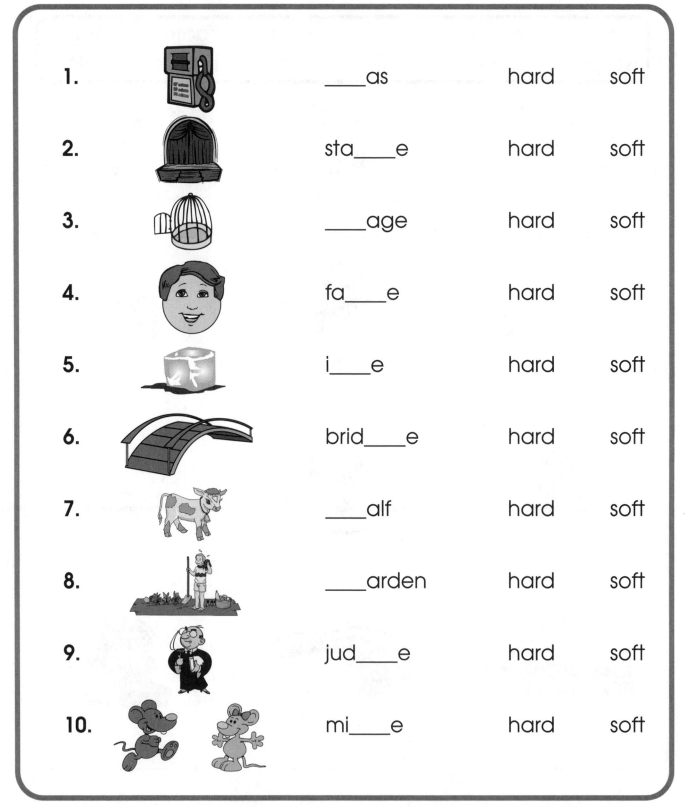

1. ____as   hard   soft

2. sta____e   hard   soft

3. ____age   hard   soft

4. fa____e   hard   soft

5. i____e   hard   soft

6. brid____e   hard   soft

7. ____alf   hard   soft

8. ____arden   hard   soft

9. jud____e   hard   soft

10. mi____e   hard   soft

Check Up: Hard and Soft c and g

Directions: Circle the word that best completes each sentence. Then, write the word in the blank.

1. Mom has on a _____ dress.

   leg   lace   place

2. We will drive across the _____.

   judge   fence   bridge

3. We saw a _____ at the farm.

   goat   gas   edge

4. Dad goes to work in the _____.

   ice   fence   city

5. Emily wears a _____ when it is cold.

   cow   cab   coat

6. What do you plant in your _____?

   cup   cage   garden

7. Mom does not like _____.

   edge   mice   pencil

8. The _____ is a kind man.

   judge   page   cent

Name _____

Consonant Blends With S

Directions: Write the consonant blend that shows the beginning sound of each picture name.

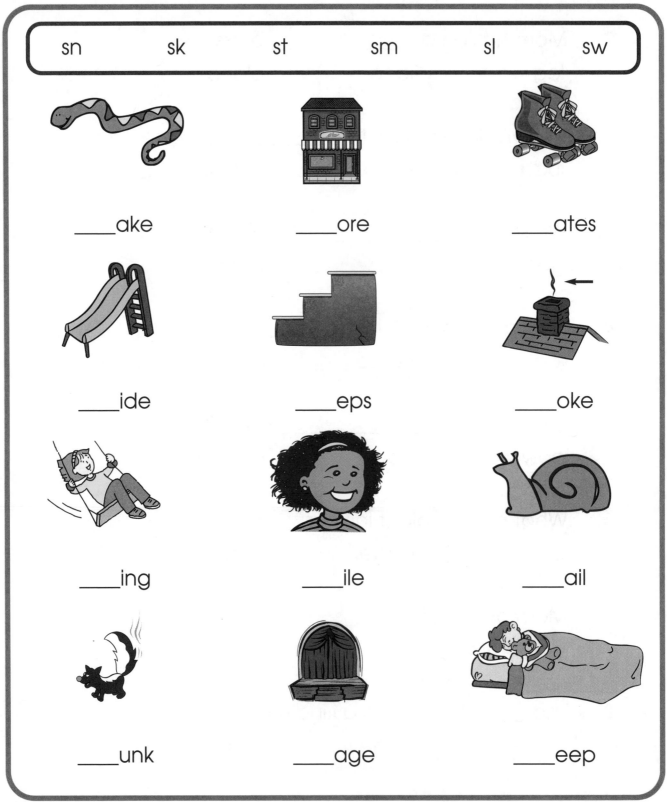

| sn | sk | st | sm | sl | sw |

___ake   ___ore   ___ates

___ide   ___eps   ___oke

___ing   ___ile   ___ail

___unk   ___age   ___eep

Consonant Blends With S

Directions: Write the word from the Word Box that names each picture.

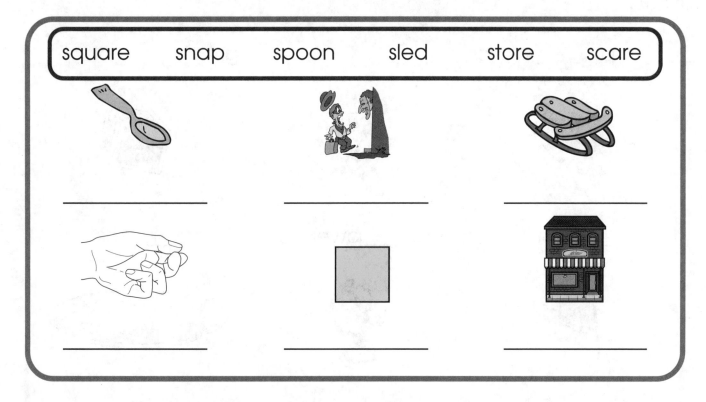

| square | snap | spoon | sled | store | scare |

_____   _____   _____

_____   _____   _____

Directions: Write two sentences. Use one word from above in each sentence.

1. _____

   _____

2. _____

   _____

Name _____

Consonant Blends With L

Directions: Write the consonant blend that shows the beginning sound of each picture name.

pl	cl	fl	gl	bl

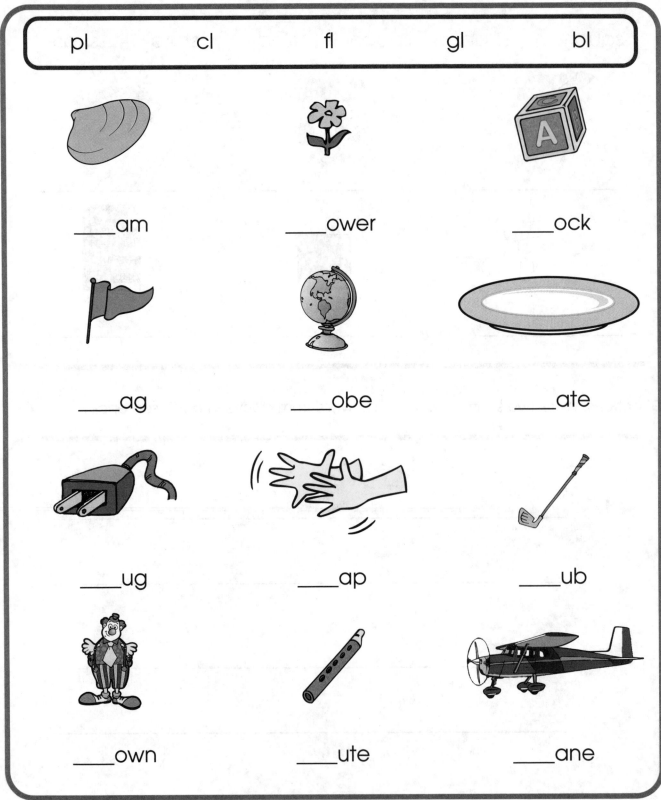

____am   ____ower   ____ock

____ag   ____obe   ____ate

____ug   ____ap   ____ub

____own   ____ute   ____ane

Consonant Blends With L

Directions: Write the word from the Word Box that names each picture.

| blow | clip | flame | glass | fly | flute |

_____   _____   _____

_____   _____   _____

Directions: Write two sentences. Use one word from above in each sentence.

1. _____

   _____

2. _____

   _____

Consonant Blends With R

Directions: Write the consonant blend that shows the beginning sound of each picture name.

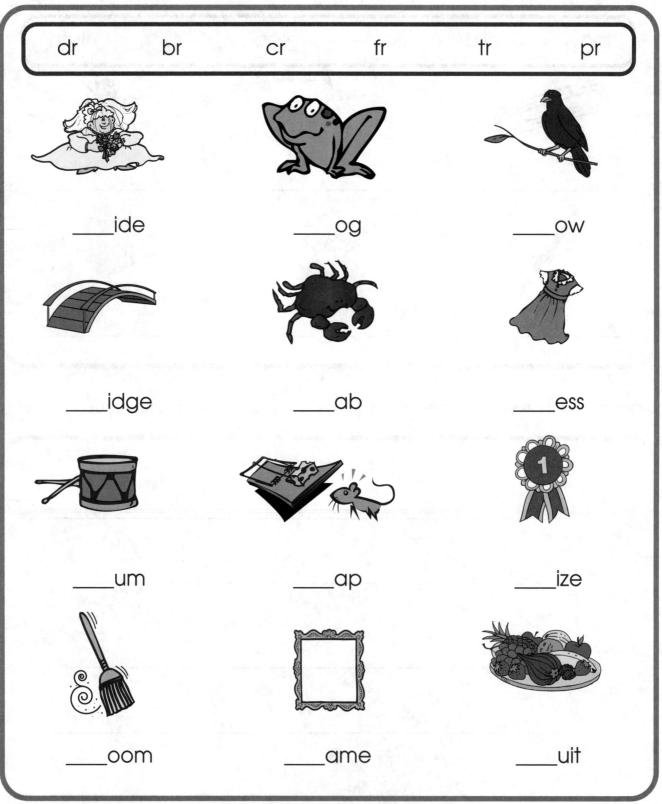

dr	br	cr	fr	tr	pr

___ide   ___og   ___ow

___idge   ___ab   ___ess

___um   ___ap   ___ize

___oom   ___ame   ___uit

Consonant Blends With R

Directions: Write the word from the Word Box that names each picture.

| crayon | tray | prince | dress | crown | tree |

_____   _____   _____

_____   _____   _____

Directions: Write two sentences. Use one word from above in each sentence.

1. _____

_____

2. _____

_____

Review: Consonant Blends

Directions: Write the word from the Word Box that names each picture.

| bridge | stage | snake | grass | tree | crab |
| crown | sled | globe | flag | plug | bride |

_____   _____   _____

_____   _____   _____

_____   _____   _____

_____   _____   _____

Final Consonant Blends

Directions: Write the final consonant blend for each word. Then, write each word again.

1. ca_____ _____

2. de_____ _____

3. roa_____ _____

4. toa_____ _____

5. ma_____ _____

Directions: Write the word that rhymes with each word below.

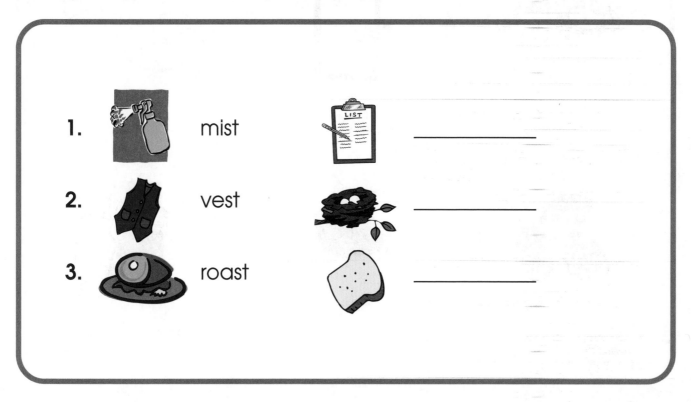

1. mist _____

2. vest _____

3. roast _____

Final Consonant Blends

Directions: Circle the consonant blend that you hear at the end of each picture name.

st   sk   st   sk   st   sk

st   sk   st   sk   st   sk

st   sk   st   sk   st   sk

st   sk   st   sk   st   sk

Name _____

Review: Final Consonant Blends

Directions: Write the word from the Word Box that names each picture.

mask	list	vest	desk	fist	mist
chest	tusk	roast	nest	crust	toast

Final Consonant Blends

Directions: Write the final consonant blend of each word. Then, write each word again.

1.   sta_____   _____

2.   pai_____   _____

3.   sku_____   _____

4.   pla_____   _____

5.   ce_____   _____

Directions: Write a word that rhymes with each word below.

1.   band   _____

2.   stump   _____

3.   sink   _____

Final Consonant Blends

Directions: Circle the word that names each picture.

pond
point
paint

bank
crank
cent

stand
cent
tent

pump
paint
plant

lamp
pump
stump

wink
sink
wind

band
bank
pond

ant
stand
and

stump
stamp
stand

stump
pond
pump

Review: Final Consonant Blends

Directions: Write the word from the Word Box that names each picture.

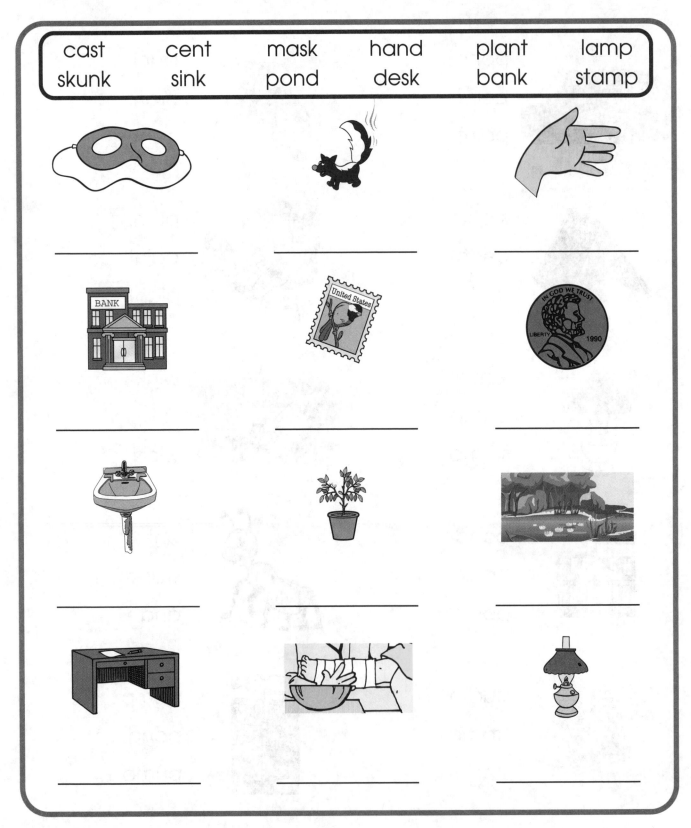

cast	cent	mask	hand	plant	lamp
skunk	sink	pond	desk	bank	stamp

_____   _____   _____

_____   _____   _____

_____   _____   _____

_____   _____   _____

Final Consonant Blends

Directions: Write the final consonant blend to complete each word. Then, write each word again.

1. ra_____   _____

2. qui_____   _____

3. wo_____   _____

4. wi_____   _____

5. go_____   _____

Directions: Write the word that rhymes with each word below.

1. shelf   _____

2. lift   _____

3. melt   _____

Name _____

Final Consonant Blends

Directions: Circle the word that names each picture.

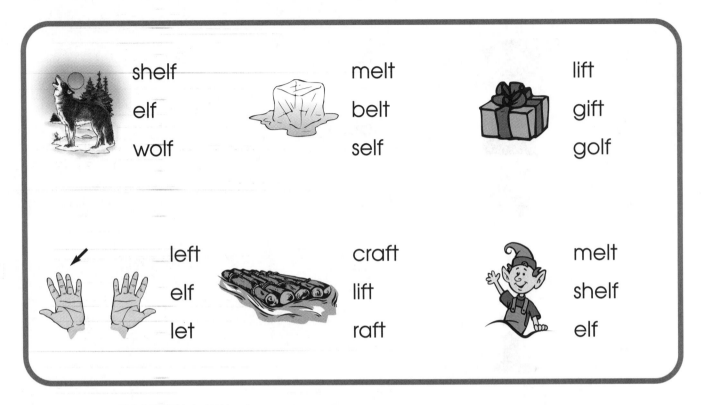

shelf	melt	lift
elf	belt	gift
wolf	self	golf
left	craft	melt
elf	lift	shelf
let	raft	elf

Directions: Write two sentences. Use one word that you circled above in each sentence.

1. _____

_____

2. _____

_____

Review: Final Consonant Blends

Directions: Write the word from the Word Box that names each picture.

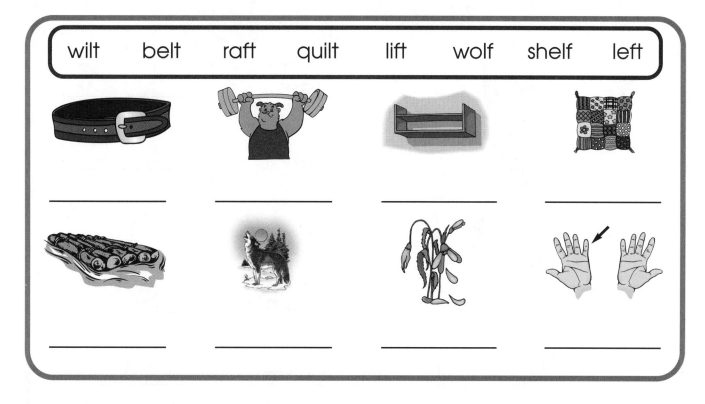

| wilt | belt | raft | quilt | lift | wolf | shelf | left |

_____   _____   _____   _____

_____   _____   _____   _____

Directions: Look at the picture and write the word that best completes each sentence.

1.   The _____ is very small.

2.   Mom gave Dad a _____ .

3.   Do you play _____ ?

4.   Put the books on the _____ .

5.   The ice will _____ in the sun.

Three-Letter Consonant Blends

Directions: Write a three-letter consonant blend to complete each word. Then, write each word again.

1. _____eet _____

2. _____ew _____

3. _____it _____

4. _____eam _____

5. _____eam _____

6. _____ub _____

7. _____ash _____

8. _____ing _____

9. _____ap _____

10. _____ong _____

Three-Letter Consonant Blends

Directions: Draw a picture to go with each word below. Then, write a sentence that tells about each picture. Make sure to use the word in the sentence.

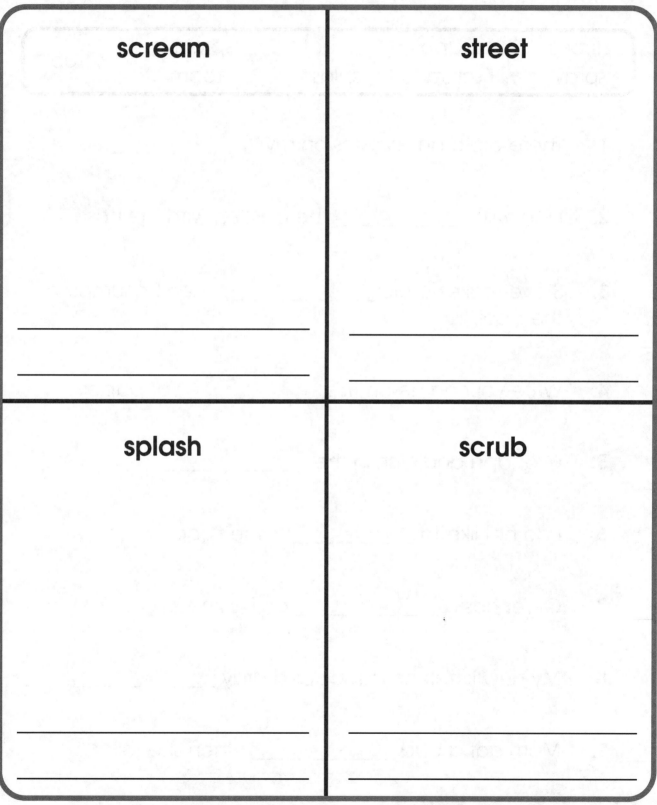

scream

_____

_____

street

_____

_____

splash

_____

_____

scrub

_____

_____

Three-Letter Consonant Blends

Directions: Write the word from the Word Box that best completes each sentence.

stripes	scrape	street	sprain	scrub
spray	scrap	splash	stream	

1. There are many houses on my _____.

2. Dad will _____ the garden with the hose.

3. Steve makes a big _____ when he jumps in the pool.

4. Write your name on this _____ of paper.

5. Grandpa and I fish in the _____.

6. I do not like to _____ the floor.

7. Oliver has a _____ on his knee.

8. My new kitten has black and gray _____.

9. Mom got a bad _____ when she fell.

Review: 3-Letter Consonant Blends

Directions: Write the word from the Word Box that names each picture.

| scream | stripes | strap | street | strong | scrub |
| screw | spring | string | split | splash | stream |

Check Up: Consonant Blends

Directions: Write a consonant blend to complete each word.

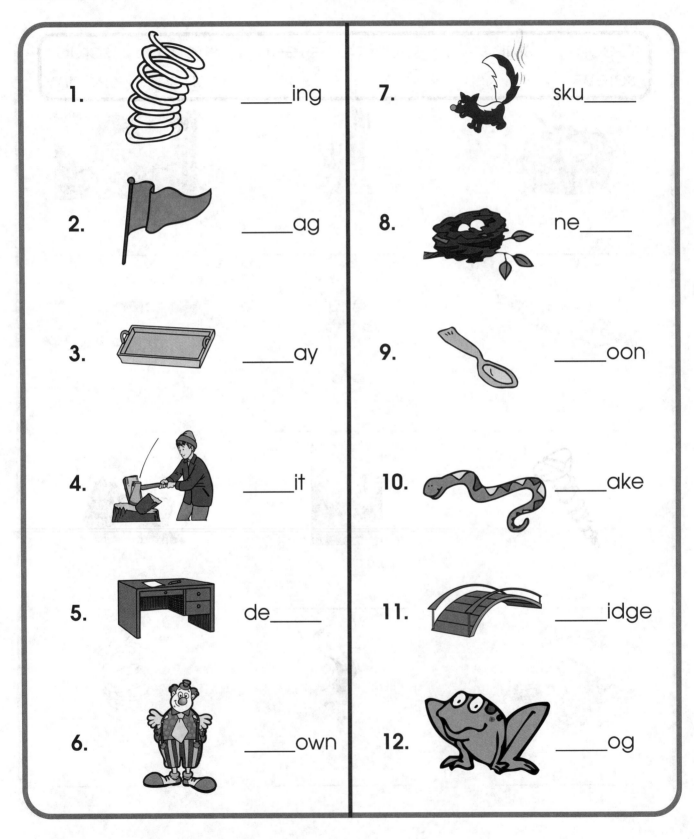

1. _____ing

2. _____ag

3. _____ay

4. _____it

5. de_____

6. _____own

7. sku_____

8. ne_____

9. _____oon

10. _____ake

11. _____idge

12. _____og

Silent Consonants

Directions: Write **kn** or **wr** to show the letters that make the beginning sound of each picture name.

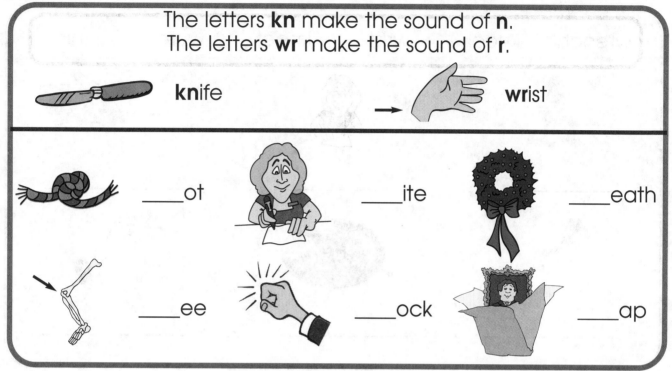

The letters **kn** make the sound of **n**.
The letters **wr** make the sound of **r**.

knife   **wr**ist

___ot   ___ite   ___eath

___ee   ___ock   ___ap

Directions: Write two sentences. Use one word from above in each sentence.

1. _____

   _____

2. _____

   _____

Silent Consonants

Directions: Write the word from the Word Box that names each picture.

| wrench | knock | wrist | kneel | write | knit |

_____   _____   _____

_____   _____   _____

Directions: Write two sentences. Use one word from above in each sentence.

1. _____

_____

2. _____

_____

Silent Consonants

Directions: Write the word from the Word Box that best completes each sentence.

knot	write	wrap	knife	
know	knock	knee	knit	wrong

1. Can you _____ this gift for Mom?

2. I _____ how to swim.

3. T.J. likes to _____ letters.

4. I fell and hurt my _____.

5. The telephone call was a _____ number.

6. Grandma wants to _____ a scarf for me.

7. There was a _____ in the rope.

8. I hear a _____ at the door.

9. Put a _____ and fork on the table.

Silent Consonants

Directions: Write the word from the Word Box that names each picture.

The letters **ck** make the sound of **k**.

du**ck**

rock	dock	pocket	brick	
jacket	clock	rocket	tack	truck

Silent Consonants

Directions: Draw a picture to go with each word below. Then, write a sentence that tells about each picture. Make sure to use the word in the sentence.

pocket	rocket
_____	_____
_____	_____
truck	rock
_____	_____
_____	_____

Silent Consonants

Directions: Write the word from the Word Box that best completes each sentence.

pack	duck	snack	chicks	dock
clock	tricks	lock	black	

1. Did you hear that _____ quack?

2. My _____ shows the wrong time.

3. Grandma has baby _____ at the farm.

4. Dad gave me a _____ for my bike.

5. My dog has _____ and white fur.

6. Mom steered the boat to the _____.

7. Dave put his books in his _____.

8. Matt likes to play _____ on his friends.

9. I am hungry for a _____.

Silent Consonants

Directions: Write the word from the Word Box that names each picture.

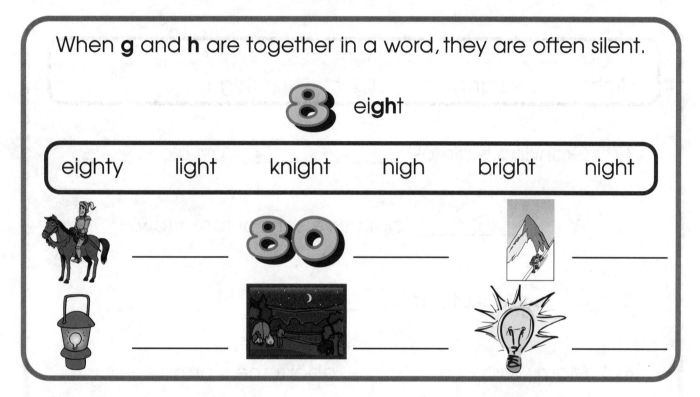

When **g** and **h** are together in a word, they are often silent.

8 ei**gh**t

| eighty | light | knight | high | bright | night |

Directions: Write two sentences. Use one word from above in each sentence.

1. _____

   _____

2. _____

   _____

Silent Consonants

Directions: Write the word from the Word Box that best completes each sentence.

might	right	fight	night	
tight	eighty	light	high	sight

1. Grandpa is almost _____ years old.

2. We _____ not have school tomorrow.

3. My red jacket is too _____.

4. Mom was _____ about the storm.

5. The snowy trees are a pretty _____.

6. The _____ is very bright.

7. It rained all _____ long.

8. I can't reach that _____ shelf.

9. Dad doesn't like it when we _____.

Review: Silent Consonants

Directions: Write a sentence that tells about each picture.

1. _____

   _____

2. _____

   _____

3. _____

   _____

4. _____

   _____

5. _____

   _____

6. _____

   _____

Check Up: Silent Consonants

Directions: Write the word from the Word Box that names each picture.

| chicks | rock | lock | knit | knight | knock |
| wrist | write | pocket | wrap | knot | light |

Vowel Pairs: AI and AY

Directions: The vowel pairs **ai** and **ay** can make the long **a** sound. Write the word that rhymes with each word below.

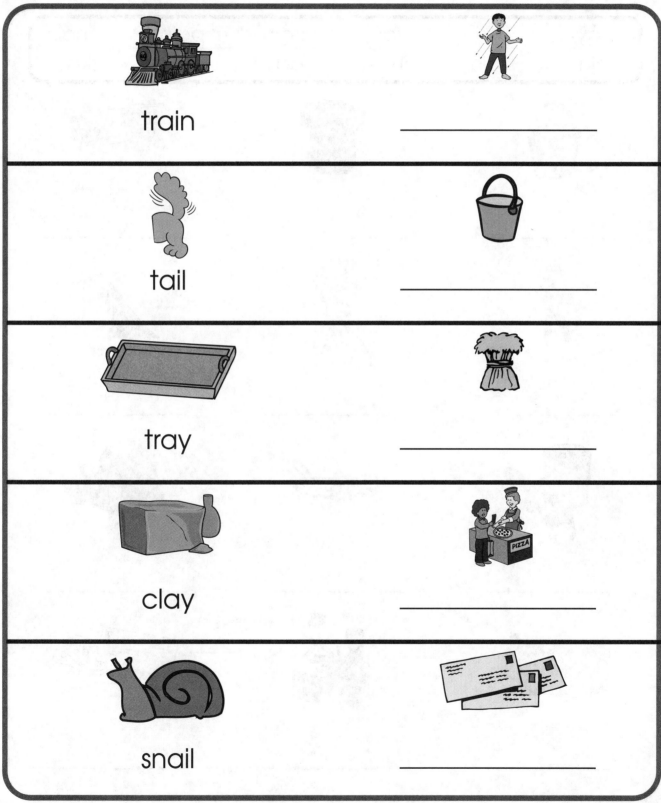

train

_____

tail

_____

tray

_____

clay

_____

snail

_____

Vowel Pairs: AI and AY

Directions: Write the word from the Word Box that names each picture.

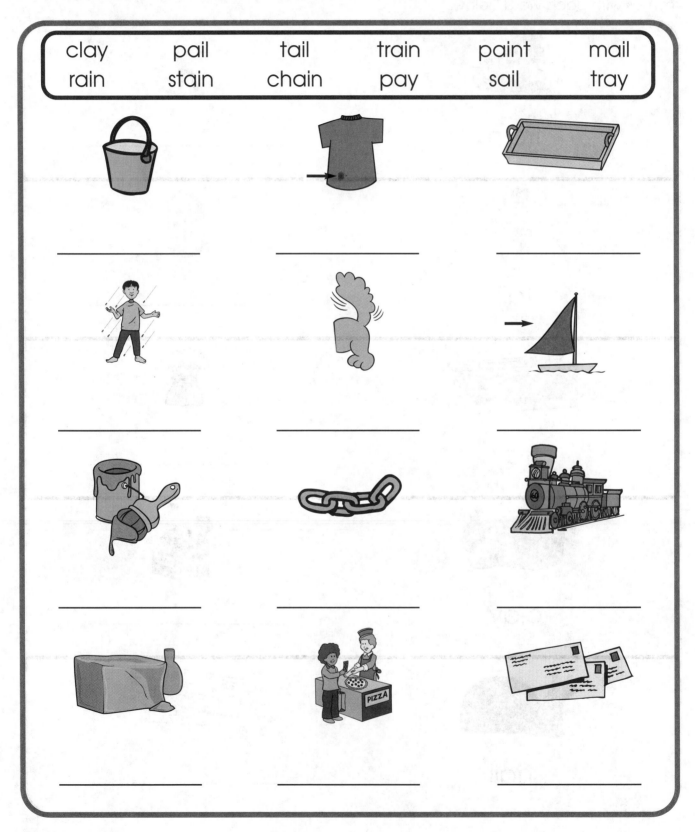

clay   pail   tail   train   paint   mail

rain   stain   chain   pay   sail   tray

_____ _____ _____

_____ _____ _____

_____ _____ _____

_____ _____ _____

Name _____

Vowel Pairs: AI and AY

Directions: Write the word from the Word Box that best completes each sentence.

paint	tray	mail	snail	hay
rain	tail	clay	train	

1. The _____ is in its shell.

2. Dad brought us cookies on a _____.

3. The cows eat _____.

4. Kelly made a bowl from _____.

5. We don't like to play outside in the _____.

6. Fluffy wags his _____ when he is happy.

7. What color _____ should we use?

8. Grandma took the _____ when she came to see us.

9. I bring in the _____ every day.

Vowel Pairs: EE and EA

Directions: The vowel pairs **ee** and **ea** can make the long **e** sound. Write the word from the Word Box that names each picture.

beads   tree   seal   bee   feet   seat

_____   _____   _____

_____   _____   _____

Directions: Write two sentences. Use one word from above in each sentence.

1. _____

_____

2. _____

_____

Vowel Pairs: EE and EA

Directions: Draw a picture to go with each word below. Then, write a sentence that tells about each picture. Make sure to use the word in the sentence.

leaf	beach
_____ _____	_____ _____
feet	sleep
_____ _____	_____ _____

Vowel Pairs: EE and EA

Directions: The vowel pair **ea** can also make the short **e** sound, as in *head*. Write the word from the Word Box that best completes each sentence.

bread	leak	steam	beak	sleep
beach	sheep	head	leap	

1. Our kitchen sink has a _____.

2. Do you like to swim at the _____?

3. The frog can _____ over the log.

4. Mom likes to bake wheat _____.

5. The bird has a very sharp _____.

6. A baby _____ is called a lamb.

7. James hit his _____ on the shelf.

8. Ryan and Eric will _____ in the tent tonight.

9. I see _____ coming from the teakettle.

Vowel Pairs: OA and OW

Directions: The vowel pairs **oa** and **ow** can make the long **o** sound. Write the word from the Word Box that names each picture.

| pillow | goat | snow | road | crow | soap |

_____   _____   _____

_____   _____   _____

Directions: Write two sentences. Use one word from above in each sentence.

1. _____

_____

2. _____

_____

Vowel Pairs: OA and OW

Directions: Draw a picture to go with each word below. Then, write a sentence that tells about each picture. Make sure to use the word in the sentence.

coat	window
_____ _____	_____ _____
bowl	**toad**
_____ _____	_____ _____

Name _____

Vowel Pairs: OA and OW

Directions: Write the word from the Word Box that best completes each sentence.

toad	row	grown	goat	
bowl	throw	toast	coat	pillow

1. A baby _____ is called a kid.

2. Can you _____ the ball to Amy?

3. I left my new wool _____ at school.

4. Mom gave me a soft _____.

5. That _____ has bumpy skin.

6. Let's make a _____ of popcorn.

7. The baby has _____ a lot in three months.

8. Dad made eggs and _____ for breakfast.

9. We can _____ the boat into the middle of the lake.

Name _____

Review: Vowel Pairs

Directions: Write the missing vowel pair for each word. Then, write each word again.

1.   b____k   _____

2.   h____   _____

3.   s____p   _____

4.   br____d   _____

5.   sl____p   _____

6.   b____l   _____

7.   s____l   _____

8.   sn____l   _____

9.   l____f   _____

10. cr____   _____

Vowel Pair: OO

Directions: The vowel pair **oo** can make a short sound, as in *hook*, and a long sound, as in *moon*. Write the word that rhymes with each word below.

spoon   _____

book   _____

spool   _____

wood   _____

stools   _____

Vowel Pair: OO

Directions: Write the word from the Word Box that names each picture.

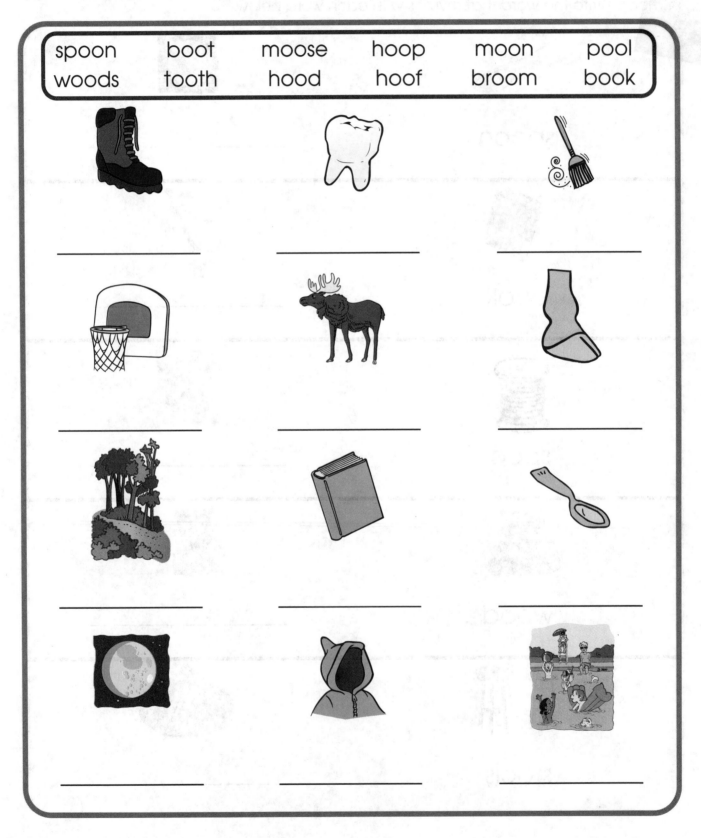

| spoon | boot | moose | hoop | moon | pool |
| woods | tooth | hood | hoof | broom | book |

Name _____

Vowel Pairs: AU and AW

Directions: The vowel pairs **au** and **aw** can make the sound that you hear in the middle of the words *cause* and *lawn*. In each row, write the two words that rhyme with the first word in the row.

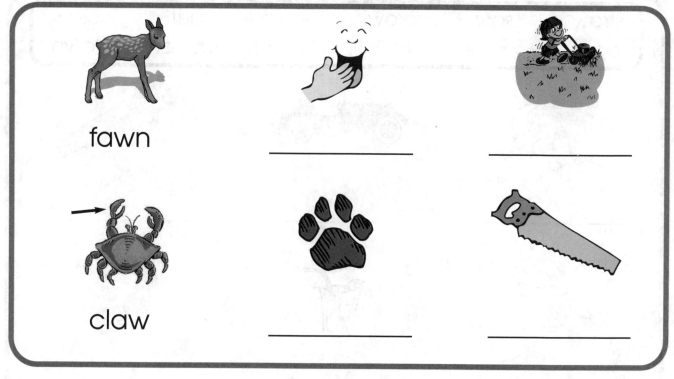

fawn

_____

_____

claw

_____

_____

Directions: Draw lines to match the words and pictures.

sauce   laundry   faucet   auto

Vowel Pairs: AU and AW

Directions: Write the word from the Word Box that names each picture.

| straw | saw | crawl | fawn | auto | claw |
| paw | sauce | yawn | faucet | laundry | lawn |

_____   _____   _____

_____   _____   _____

_____   _____   _____

Vowel Pairs: AU and AW

Directions: Write the word from the Word Box that best completes each sentence.

fawn	caught	straw	auto	lawn
faucet	crawl	shawl	saw	

1. Dad put a new _____ on the sink.

2. A baby deer is called a _____.

3. Mom cut the wood with a _____.

4. My baby brother is just learning to _____.

5. The fish got _____ in the net.

6. Our family bought a new car at the _____ show.

7. The _____ is nice and green in the spring.

8. Grandma wears a _____ to keep warm.

9. Ryan sips his milk through a _____.

Vowel Pair: EW

Directions: The vowel pair **ew** can make the long **u** sound. Write the word from the Word Box that names each picture.

news	stew	jewelry	screw

1. _____

3. _____

2. _____

4. _____

Directions: Write two sentences. Use one word from the Word Box in each sentence.

flew	new	few	grew

1. _____

_____

2. _____

_____

Vowel Pair: EW

Directions: Write the word from the Word Box that best completes each sentence.

chew	grew	dew	jewelry	
drew	few	flew	news	stew

1. Last year, we _____ beans in our garden.

2. We went to the beach a _____ times this summer.

3. There is _____ on the lawn in the morning.

4. Have you heard the good _____?

5. Mom made beef _____ for dinner.

6. Mary _____ a picture of Mom.

7. Murphey likes to _____ on a bone.

8. Mom likes to wear _____.

9. The bird _____ high in the sky.

Review: Vowel Pairs

Directions: Write the word from the Word Box that names each picture.

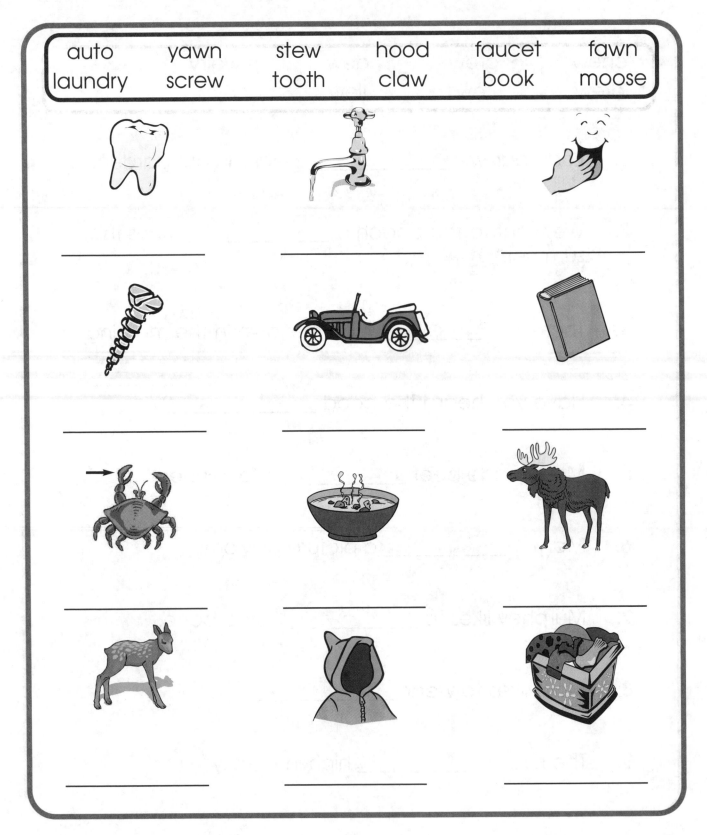

| auto | yawn | stew | hood | faucet | fawn |
| laundry | screw | tooth | claw | book | moose |

The Sounds of Y

Directions: Read the words. Write each word in the correct column.

Sometimes **y** can sound like long **e**,
and sometimes it can sound like long **i**.

puppy

fry

dry

baby

city

sky

pony

fly

bunny

cry

Y as Long e	Y as Long i
_____	_____
_____	_____
_____	_____
_____	_____

The Sounds of Y

Directions: Write the word from the Word Box that names each picture.

| bunny | fly | cry | money | muddy | city |
| puppy | sky | baby | fry | key | dry |

_____   _____   _____

_____   _____   _____

_____   _____   _____

_____   _____   _____

Name _____

The Sounds of Y

Directions: Write the word from the Word Box that best completes each sentence.

silly	cry	city	story	
try	muddy	happy	fry	puppy

1. Can you hear the baby _____?

2. The _____ is a busy place.

3. Dad will _____ not to be late.

4. It is _____ after it rains.

5. My brother takes good care of his new _____.

6. Elise is _____ when she reads.

7. Molly will read us a _____.

8. Josh told us a _____ joke.

9. Do you know how to _____ an egg?

Name _____

Check Up: Vowel Pairs and Sounds of Y

Directions: Write the name of each picture.

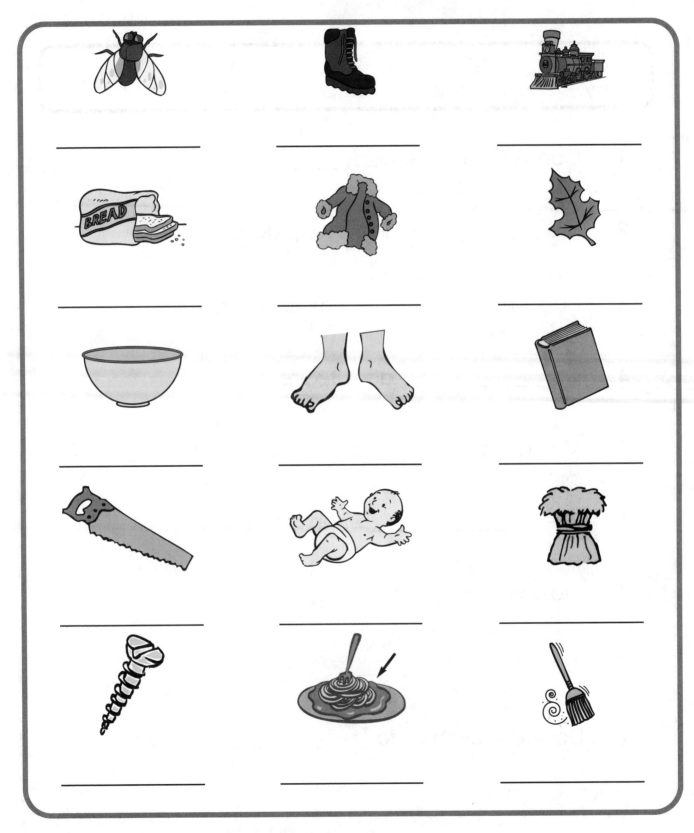

Name _____

Consonant Pairs

Directions: Write the letters **sh**, **ch**, **th**, or **wh** to complete each word. Then, write each word again.

1. _____op _____

2. _____read _____

3. _____ell _____

4. _____ree _____

5. _____ale _____

6. _____ain _____

7. _____in _____

8. _____icks _____

9. _____eel _____

10. _____oe _____

Consonant Pairs

Directions: Write the word from the Word Box that names each picture.

wheel	ship	chair	whale	shoe	shelf
think	cheese	throat	thread	cheek	thin

_____   _____   _____

_____   _____   _____

_____   _____   _____

_____   _____   _____

Final Consonant Pairs

Directions: Write the final consonant pair **sh**, **ch**, **tch**, **th**, or **ng** to complete each word. Then, write each word again.

1. ri____   _____

2. spri____   _____

3. di____   _____

4. bran____   _____

5. chur____   _____

6. stri____   _____

7. ba____   _____

8. bru____   _____

9. wi____   _____

10. too____   _____

Final Consonant Pairs and Blends

Directions: Write the word that rhymes with each word below.

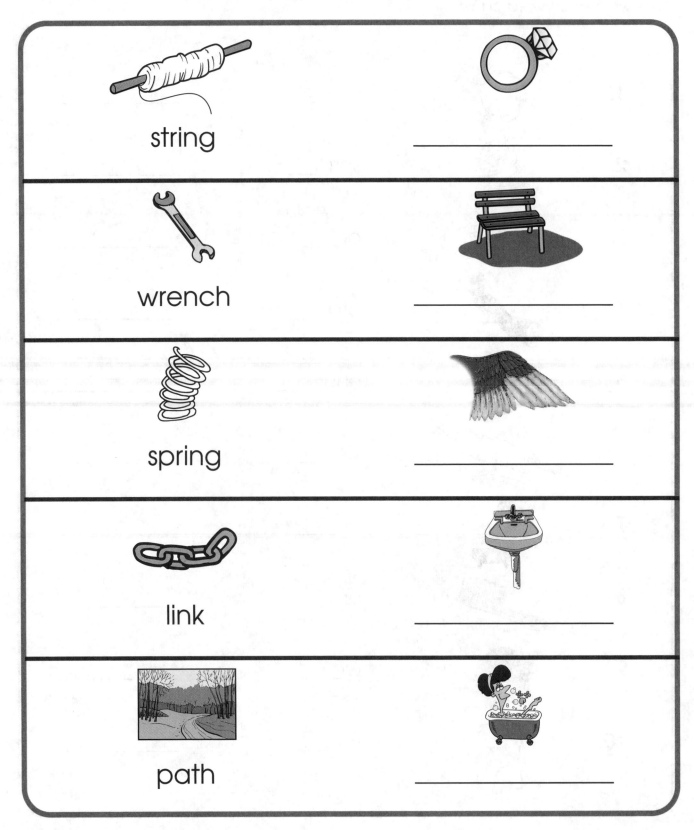

string _____

wrench _____

spring _____

link _____

path _____

Review: Consonant Pairs and Blends

Directions: Write the word from the Word Box that names each picture.

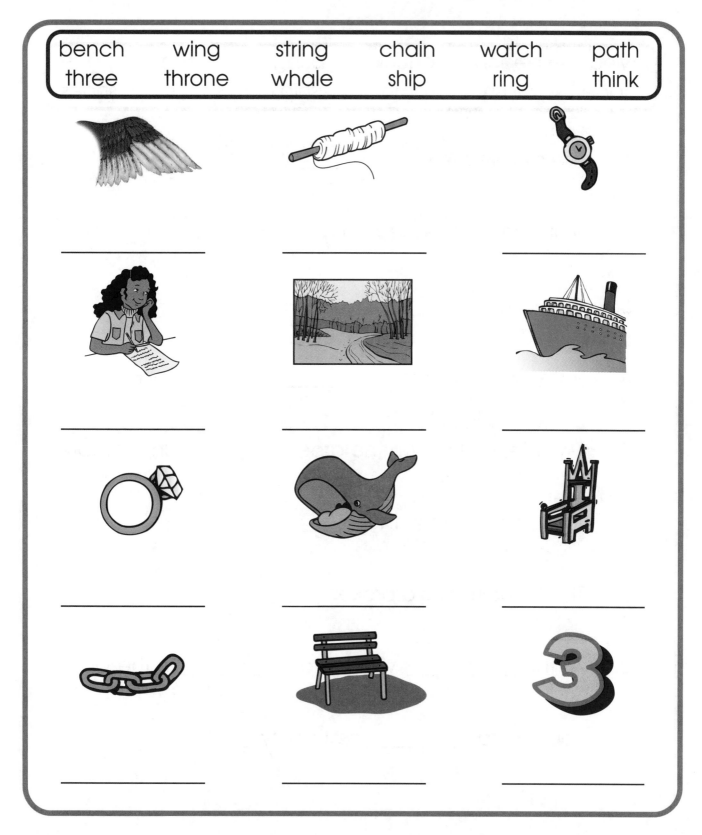

bench   wing   string   chain   watch   path
three   throne   whale   ship   ring   think

Check Up: Consonant Pairs and Blends

Directions: Write the word or words from the Word Box that best completes each sentence.

wing	beach	chunk	bring	bench	cheese
shade	wash	path	ship	splash	shoes

1. The mouse ate a _____ of _____.

2. Mom and Dad sailed on a _____.

3. Can you _____ a snack to the picnic?

4. Patty walked on the _____ in the woods.

5. My sister is sitting on the green _____ in the park.

6. To stay cool, I sit in the _____.

7. The bluebird has a broken _____.

8. At the _____, we like to _____ in the water.

9. You should _____ your dirty _____.

Name _____

Vowels With R: AR and ER

Directions: Write the word from the Word Box that names each picture.

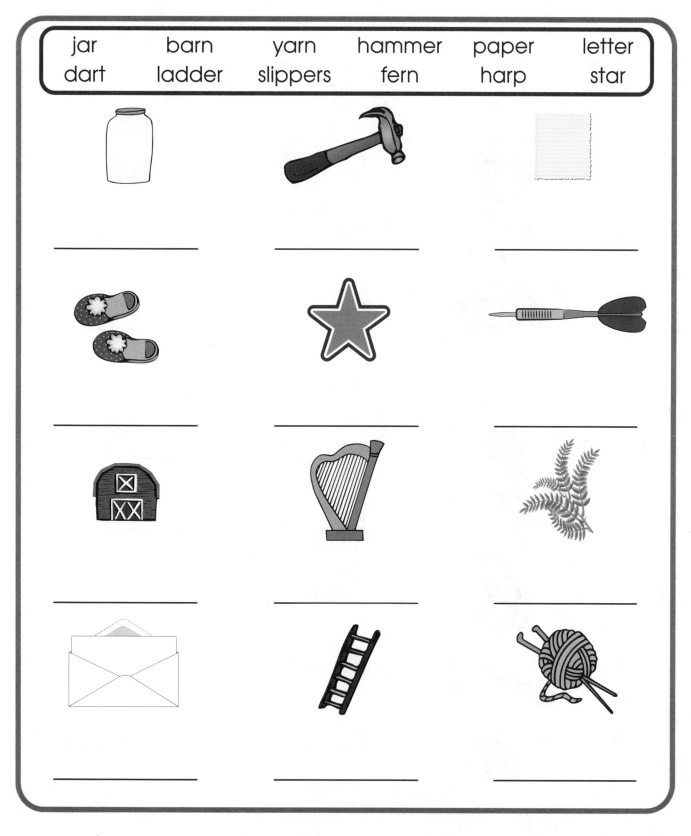

jar	barn	yarn	hammer	paper	letter
dart	ladder	slippers	fern	harp	star

Vowels With R: AR and ER

Directions: Write the missing letters **ar** or **er** for each word. Then, write each word again.

1. danc_____ _____

2. f_____m _____

3. slipp_____s _____

4. c_____ _____

5. lett_____ _____

6. y_____n _____

7. p_____k _____

8. camp_____ _____

9. hamm_____ _____

10. st_____ _____

Vowels With R: IR and OR

Directions: Write the word from the Word Box that names each picture.

dirt	thorn	bird	girl	corn	fort
storm	cork	thirty	fork	shirt	skirt

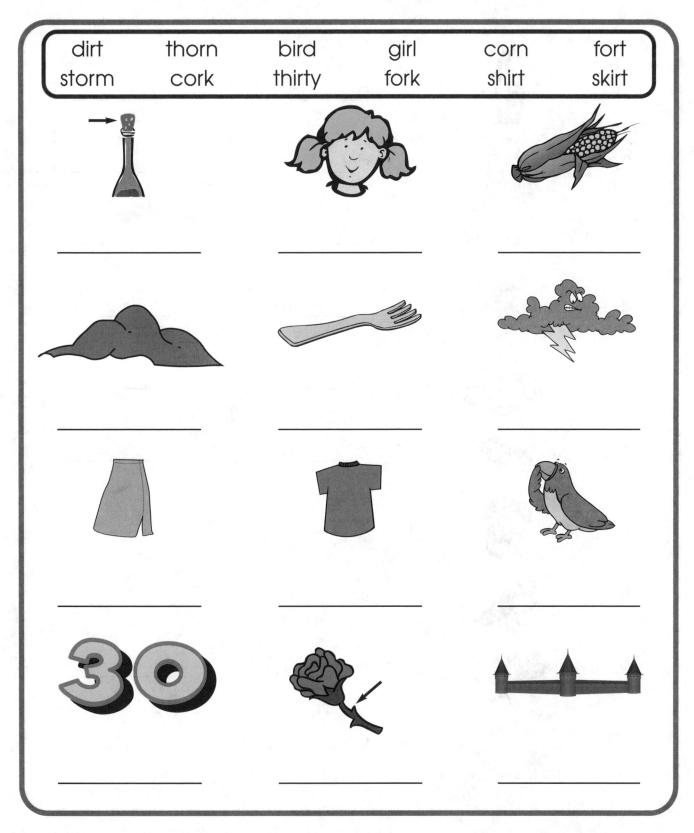

_____ _____ _____

_____ _____ _____

_____ _____ _____

_____ _____ _____

Name _____

Vowels With R: IR and OR

Directions: Write the missing letters **ir** or **or** for each word. Then, write each word again.

1.   h_____se   _____

2.   sk_____t   _____

3.   f_____k   _____

4.   st_____m   _____

5.   g_____l   _____

6.   c_____n   _____

7.   sh_____t   _____

8.   b_____d   _____

9.   th_____n   _____

10. c_____d   _____

Name _____

Vowels With R: UR

Directions: Write the word from the Word Box that names each picture.

hurt	fur	turn	burn	curb

_____   _____   _____

_____   _____

Directions: Write two sentences. Use one word from above in each sentence.

1. _____

_____

2. _____

_____

Name _____

Vowels With R

Directions: Write the word that rhymes with each word below.

horn _____

car _____

turn _____

shirt _____

thorn _____

Vowels With R

Directions: Write the word from the Word Box that best completes each sentence.

bird	fur	corn	fern	
cart	barn	hurt	bark	horn

1. The bear's _____ keeps it warm.

2. That _____ is a very pretty plant.

3. Grandpa put the hay in the _____.

4. Grandma ate _____ on the cob for dinner.

5. I _____ my foot playing soccer.

6. Fido will _____ when he wants a bone.

7. The _____ has four wheels.

8. I found a baby _____ in its nest.

9. My sister plays the _____ in the school band.

Review: Vowels With R

Directions: Write the word from the Word Box that names each picture.

| fork | shirt | hurt | bird | star | burn |
| letter | turn | fern | horn | car | barn |

_____   _____   _____

_____   _____   _____

_____   _____   _____

_____   _____   _____

Check Up: Vowels With R

Directions: Write six sentences. Use one word from the Word Box in each sentence.

letter	fork	bird	farm	horn	barn

1. _____

_____

2. _____

_____

3. _____

_____

4. _____

_____

5. _____

_____

6. _____

_____

Vowel Pairs: OI and OY

Directions: The vowel pairs **oi** and **oy** can make the sound that you hear in the middle of the words *noise* and *boys*. Write the word from the Word Box that names each picture.

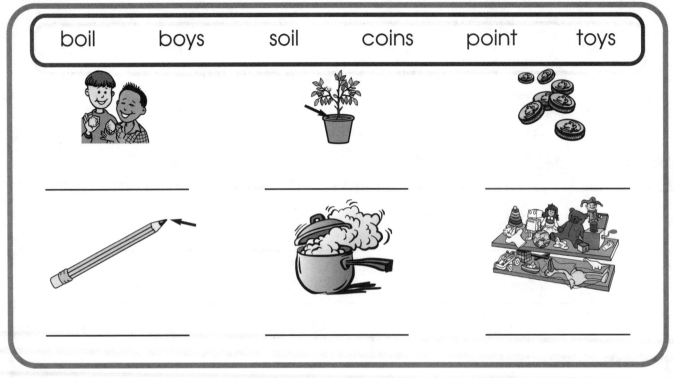

| boil | boys | soil | coins | point | toys |

Directions: Write two sentences. Use one word from above in each sentence.

1. _____

   _____

2. _____

   _____

Vowel Pairs: OI and OY

Directions: Write the missing letters **oi** or **oy** for each word. Then, write the word again.

1. b_____l _____

2. c_____ns _____

3. b_____s _____

4. s_____l _____

5. _____ster _____

6. _____l _____

7. t_____s _____

8. p_____nt _____

Vowel Pairs: OI and OY

Directions: Write the word from the Word Box that best completes each sentence.

boys	voice	enjoys	noise	point
soil	join	toys	coins	

1. Her loud _____ hurts my ears.

2. I broke the _____ on my pencil.

3. How many _____ do you have in your pocket?

4. We gave the baby two new _____ to play with.

5. Our car is making a funny _____.

6. Those _____ are friends from school.

7. Mark is going to _____ the reading club.

8. We got the _____ ready so we could plant our garden.

9. Mom _____ going to the library.

Name _____

Vowel Pairs: OU and OW

Directions: The vowel pairs **ou** and **ow** can make the sound you hear in the middle of *mouth* and *clown*. Write the word from the Word Box that names each picture.

shower	pound	plow	crown	house	clown
cow	blouse	flower	bounce	frown	gown

_____ _____ _____

_____ _____ _____

_____ _____ _____

_____ _____ _____

Vowel Pairs: OU and OW

Directions: Write the missing letters **ou** or **ow** for each word. Then, write each word again.

1. cl_____d _____

2. m_____th _____

3. _____l _____

4. cl_____n _____

5. p_____nd _____

6. pl_____ _____

7. cr_____n _____

8. c_____ _____

9. fl_____er _____

10. h_____se _____

Vowel Pairs: OU and OW

Directions: Write the word from the Word Box that best completes each sentence.

cloud	mouse	clown	house	crown
blouse	ground	cow	pound	

1. The queen wears a gold _____.

2. The little _____ likes to nibble on cheese.

3. Dad uses the hammer to _____ nails.

4. The _____ did funny tricks.

5. Mom has a pretty blue _____ and skirt.

6. The _____ likes to munch on grass.

7. There is a puffy white _____ in the sky.

8. I dropped my watch on the _____.

9. My _____ is not far from school.

Review: Vowel Pairs

Directions: Write the word that rhymes with each word below.

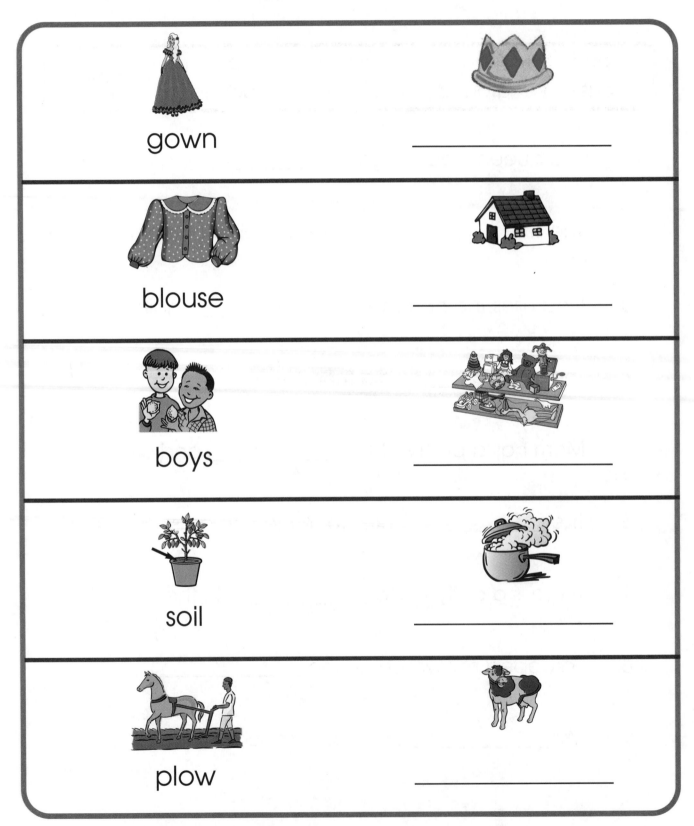

gown

_____

blouse

_____

boys

_____

soil

_____

plow

_____

Check Up: Vowel Pairs

Directions: Write a word that names each picture. Each word should have the **oi**, **oy**, **ou**, or **ow** vowel pair.

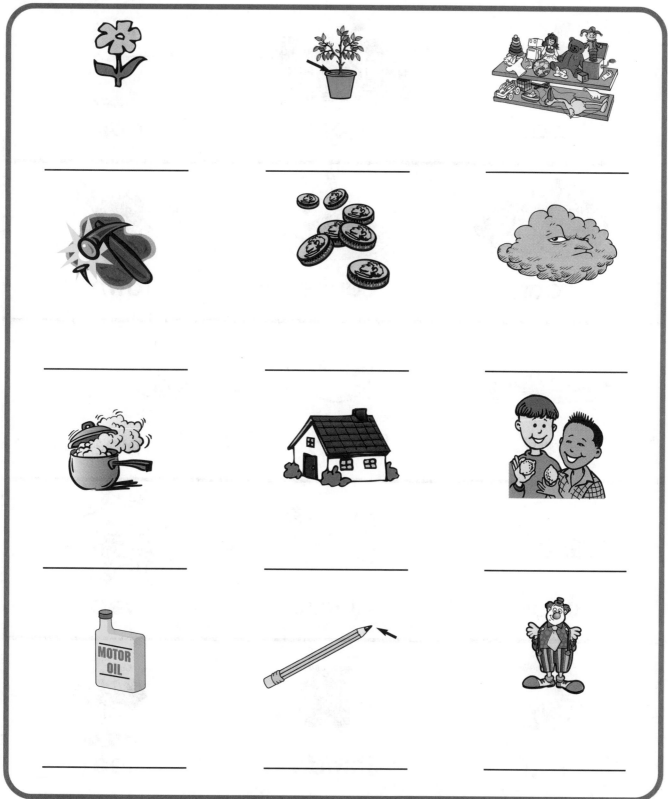

Letters and Their Sounds

bat gate pail

car sauce fawn

tray cup mice

chain chicks web

seal thread tree

Letters and Their Sounds

lett**er**

scr**ew**

game

ca**g**e

hit

f**i**ve

sk**ir**t

knee

wi**ng**

f**o**x

s**oa**p

r**o**se

oil

sp**oo**n

h**oo**k

Letters and Their Sounds

corn

house

crow

owl

boys

ship

think

throat

rug

mule

burn

whale

wrench

sky

puppy

Practice Page

Practice Page

Practice Page

Practice Page

Answer Key

Review: Beginning and Ending Sounds

Directions: Say the name of each picture. Write the missing letter or letters to complete each word.

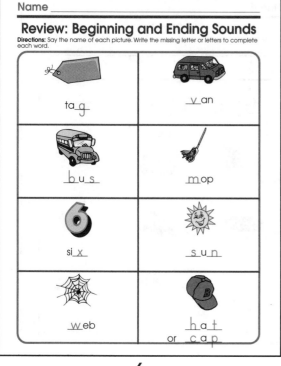

ta_g_   _v_ an

_b_ _u_ _s_   _m_ op

si_x_   _s_ _u_ _n_

_w_ eb   _h_ _a_ _t_
or _c_ _a_ _p_

6

Review: Beginning and Ending Sounds

Directions: Say the name of each picture. Write the missing letter or letters to complete each word.

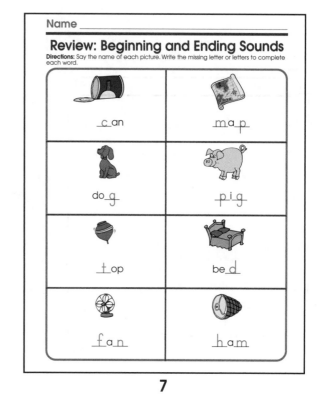

_c_ an   m_a_p

do_g_   _p_ i _g_

_t_ op   be_d_

_f_ _a_ _n_   _h_ _a_ _m_

7

Short a

Directions: Connect all the pictures whose names have the short **a** sound from the cat to the bag.

8

Short a

Directions: Write the word from the Word Box that names each picture.

| van | cab | cap | apple | map | pan |
| add | ham | ant | can | hand | ax |

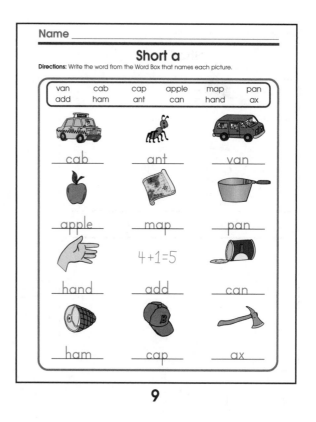

cab   ant   van

apple   map   pan

hand   add   can

ham   cap   ax

4+1=5

9

Answer Key

Short a

Directions: Write the word from the Word Box that best completes each sentence.

pan	hand	hat	has	ant	as	ham	apple	am

1. An __ant__ is very tiny.
2. Can you __hand__ Dad the bag?
3. I wear a __hat__.
4. I __am__ glad.
5. He is __as__ tall as a yardstick.
6. Mom will fry fish in a __pan__.
7. We had __ham__ for lunch.
8. She __has__ a new hat.
9. The __apple__ is red.

10

Short e

Directions: Write the word from the Word Box that names each picture.

desk	bed	net	tent	web	leg
nest	hen	egg	jet	belt	dress

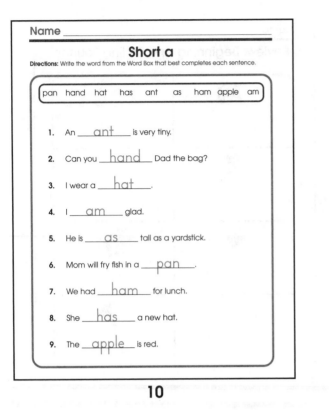

bed — egg — net

leg — hen — jet

belt — tent — desk

web — dress — nest

11

Short e

Directions: Write a word that rhymes with each word below.

Answers will vary. Examples:

1. nest — vest
2. net — bet
3. jet — wet
4. sled — bed
5. hen — pen

Directions: Draw a picture of something whose name has the short e sound. Then, write the word that names the picture.

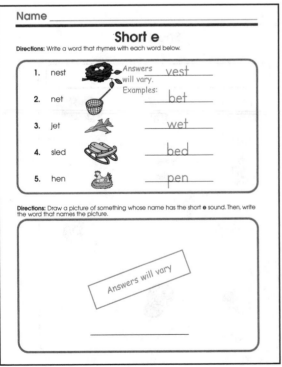

Answers will vary

12

Short e

Directions: Write the word from the Word Box that best completes each sentence.

beg	smell	net	wet	nest

1. Dad had the frog in a __net__.
2. The bird sleeps in its __nest__.
3. Can you __smell__ the flower?
4. The shirt is __wet__.
5. My dog likes to __beg__.

Directions: Write two short e words of your own. Then, use each word in a sentence.

1. _____ 2. _____

1. _____

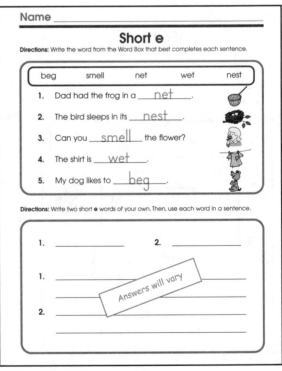

Answers will vary

2. _____

13

Spectrum Phonics Grade 2

Answer Key

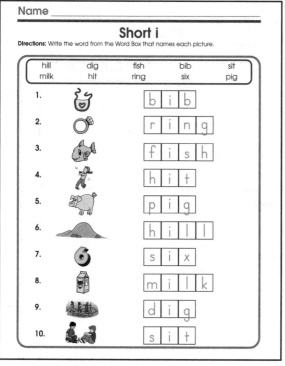

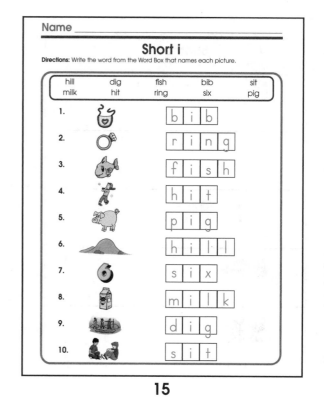

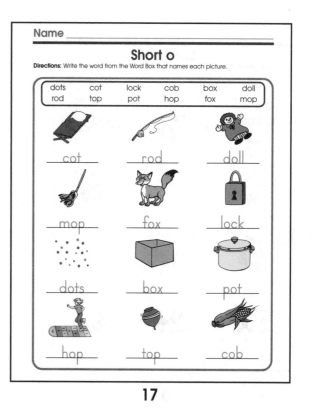

Answer Key

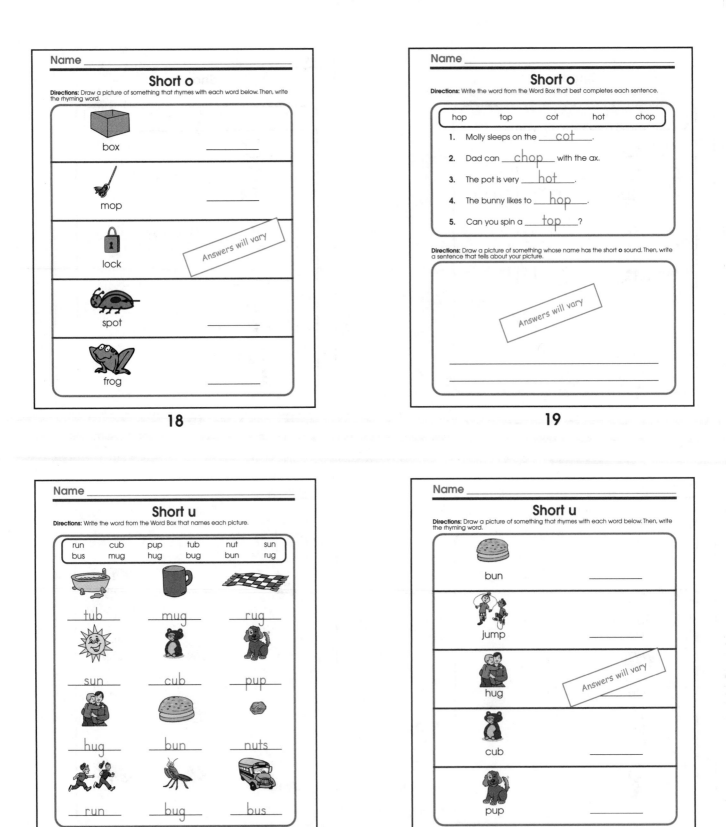

Name _____

Short o

Directions: Draw a picture of something that rhymes with each word below. Then, write the rhyming word.

box _____

mop _____

lock _____ *Answers will vary*

spot _____

frog _____

18

Name _____

Short o

Directions: Write the word from the Word Box that best completes each sentence.

hop	top	cot	hot	chop

1. Molly sleeps on the ___cot___.
2. Dad can ___chop___ with the ax.
3. The pot is very ___hot___.
4. The bunny likes to ___hop___.
5. Can you spin a ___top___?

Directions: Draw a picture of something whose name has the short **o** sound. Then, write a sentence that tells about your picture.

Answers will vary

_____
_____

19

Name _____

Short u

Directions: Write the word from the Word Box that names each picture.

run	cub	pup	tub	nut	sun
bus	mug	hug	bug	bun	rug

tub   mug   rug

sun   cub   pup

hug   bun   nuts

run   bug   bus

20

Name _____

Short u

Directions: Draw a picture of something that rhymes with each word below. Then, write the rhyming word.

bun _____

jump _____

hug _____ *Answers will vary*

cub _____

pup _____

21

Answer Key

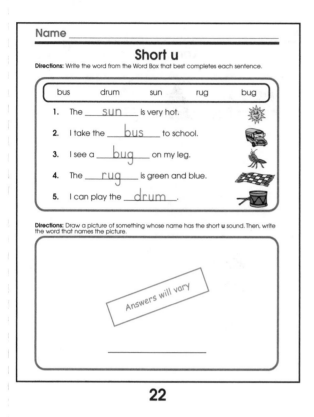
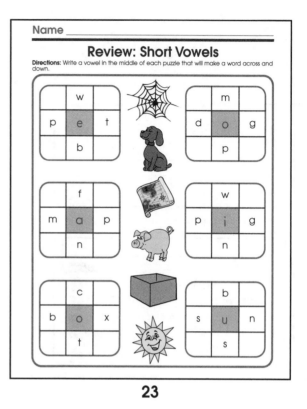
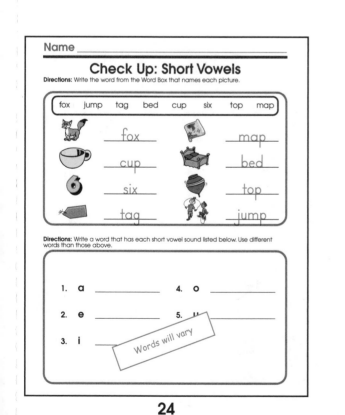
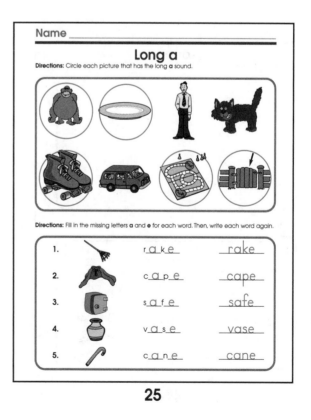

Answer Key

Name _____

Long a

Directions: Draw a picture of something that has the long **a** sound. Then, write a sentence that tells about your picture.

Answers will vary

_____

_____

Directions: Write the word from the Word Box that best completes each sentence.

ape	lake	cane	vase	bake	game

1. We swim in the __lake__.
2. Mom put flowers in the __vase__.
3. Sam plays a __game__.
4. I will __bake__ a cake.
5. Grandpa needs a __cane__ to walk.
6. We saw an __ape__ at the zoo.

26

Name _____

Long i

Directions: Draw a line to match each picture with its name.

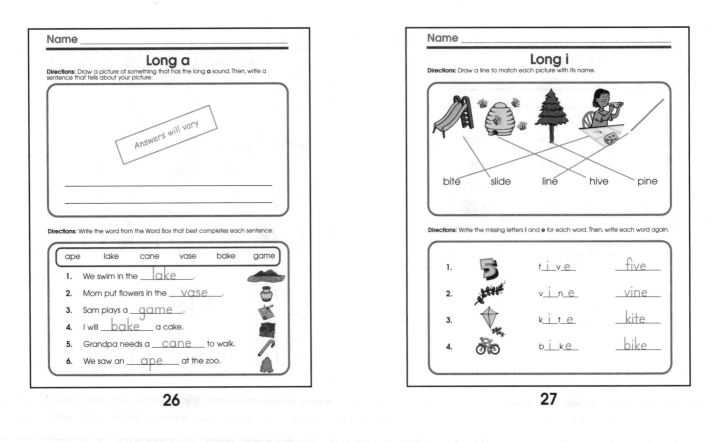

bite   slide   line   hive   pine

Directions: Write the missing letters **i** and **e** for each word. Then, write each word again.

1. f_i_v_e_   five
2. v_i_n_e_   vine
3. k_i_t_e_   kite
4. b_i_k_e_   bike

27

Name _____

Long i

Directions: Draw a picture of something that has the long **i** sound. Then, write the word that names the picture.

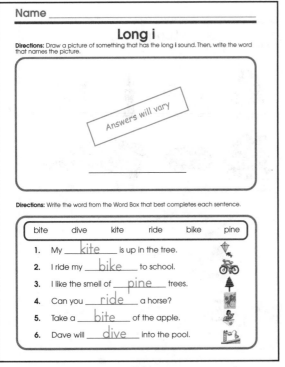

Answers will vary

_____

Directions: Write the word from the Word Box that best completes each sentence.

bite	dive	kite	ride	bike	pine

1. My __kite__ is up in the tree.
2. I ride my __bike__ to school.
3. I like the smell of __pine__ trees.
4. Can you __ride__ a horse?
5. Take a __bite__ of the apple.
6. Dave will __dive__ into the pool.

28

Name _____

Long o

Directions: Write the word from the Word Box that names each picture.

stove	cone	pole	rope	bone	nose

__cone__   __rope__   __stove__

__pole__   __nose__   __bone__

Directions: Write the missing letters **o** and **e** for each word. Then, write each word again.

1. r_o_s_e_   rose
2. gl_o_b_e_   globe
3. h_o_s_e_   hose

29

Answer Key

Long o

Directions: Write the word from the Word Box that best completes each sentence.

hose	note	rose	stove	rope	bone

1. Mom gave Dad a __rose__ .
2. Put the __rope__ in the car.
3. Spike will give Fido a __bone__ .
4. Can you sing that __note__ ?
5. Dad has a green __hose__ in the yard.
6. The __stove__ is very hot.

Directions: Write the word that names each picture below.

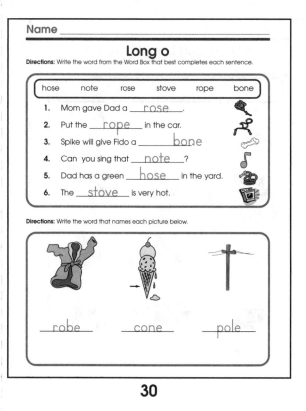

__robe__   __cone__   __pole__

30

Long u

Directions: Write the missing letters **u** and **e** for each word. Then, write each word again.

1. t __u__ n __e__   __tune__
2. m __u__ l __e__   __mule__
3. d __u__ n __e__   __dune__
4. c __u__ t __e__   __cute__
5. c __u__ b __e__   __cube__

Directions: Write a word that rhymes with each word below.

1. tube   Examples: __cube__
2. prune   __tune__
3. flute   __cute__

31

Long u

Directions: Write the missing letters **u** and **e** for each word. Then, write each word again.

1. t __u__ n __e__   __tune__
2. m __u__ l __e__   __mule__
3. d __u__ n __e__   __dune__
4. c __u__ t __e__   __cute__
5. c __u__ b __e__   __cube__

Directions: Write a word that rhymes with each word below.

1. tube   Examples: __cube__
2. prune   __tune__
3. flute   __cute__

32

Review: Long Vowels

Directions: Write the missing vowels to complete each word.

1. r __a__ k __e__
2. r __o__ b __e__
3. t __a__ p __e__
4. t __u__ b __e__
5. k __i__ t __e__

Directions: Write a word that rhymes with each word below.

Answers will vary. Examples:

1. vine __pine__   5. wave __save__
2. gate __late__   6. like __bike__
3. hose __nose__   7. tune __dune__
4. cube __tube__   8. game __tame__

33

Answer Key

Check Up: Long Vowels
Directions: Write the word from the Word Box that names each picture.

cape	safe	bike	vase	mule	bone
tube	prune	hose	cone	cube	nine

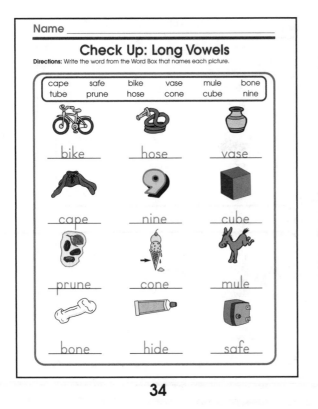

bike hose vase

cape nine cube

prune cone mule

bone hide safe

34

Short and Long Vowels
Directions: Write the word from the Word Box that names each picture.

duck	pan	rod	skates	lips	tape
cub	dress	slide	cone	vine	flute

cub cone duck

vine tape rod

pan flute dress

skate lips slide

35

Short and Long Vowels
Directions: Write each picture name in the correct column.

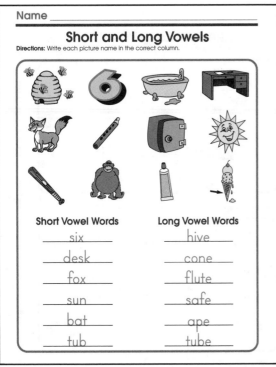

Short Vowel Words	Long Vowel Words
six	hive
desk	cone
fox	flute
sun	safe
bat	ape
tub	tube

36

Short and Long Vowels
Directions: Write the missing vowel or vowels for each word.

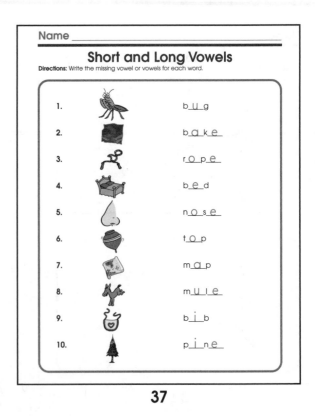

1. b u g
2. b a k e
3. r o p e
4. b e d
5. n o s e
6. t o p
7. m a p
8. m u l e
9. b i b
10. p i n e

37

Answer Key

Short and Long Vowels

Directions: Draw a picture of something whose name has the vowel sound written in each box. Then, write the word that names each picture.

Long u	Short a	Short e
_____	_____	_____

Long i	Long o	Short i
	Answers will vary	
_____	_____	_____

Short u	Long a	Short o
_____	_____	_____

38

Check Up: Short and Long Vowels

Directions: Circle the word that best completes each sentence. Then, write the word in the blank.

1. Lisa put the hat in the __box__.
   bone   (box)   robe

2. A __hog__ is a very large animal.
   hag   hose   (hog)

3. The mother bear takes care of her __cub__.
   cube   cup   (cub)

4. Let's play a __game__.
   gum   gate   (game)

5. I will play a __tune__ on the flute.
   tub   tube   (tune)

6. Put the __rope__ on the boat.
   robe   (rope)   nine

7. I like to go down the __slide__.
   five   fish   (slide)

8. He will wash the dog in the __tub__.
   (tub)   tube   tag

39

Hard and Soft c

Directions: The letter **c** can have the hard sound of **k**. It can also have the soft sound of **s**. Draw a line to match each word with its picture.

Hard **c** = calf   Soft **c** = cent

cot   ice   city   coat

Directions: Write each picture name from above in the correct column.

Hard c Words	Soft c Words
cot	city
calf	ice

40

Hard and Soft c

Directions: Write the word from the Word Box that names each picture.

pencil	city	fence	cow	ice	mice
car	cup	cent	cab	face	cap

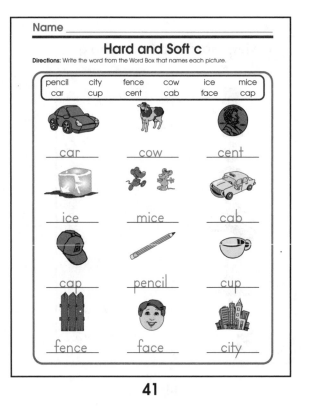

car   cow   cent

ice   mice   cab

cap   pencil   cup

fence   face   city

41

Spectrum Phonics Grade 2

137

Answer Key

Name _____

Hard and Soft g

Directions: The letter **g** can have a hard sound and a soft sound. Draw a line to match each word with its picture.

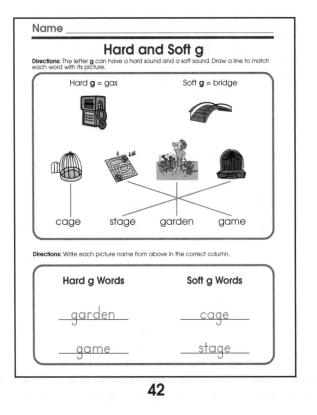

Hard **g** = gas   Soft **g** = bridge

cage   stage   garden   game

Directions: Write each picture name from above in the correct column.

Hard g Words	Soft g Words
garden	cage
game	stage

42

Name _____

Hard and Soft g

Directions: Write the word from the Word Box that names each picture.

wig	edge	judge	goat	gate	cage
stage	globe	dog	page	bridge	pig

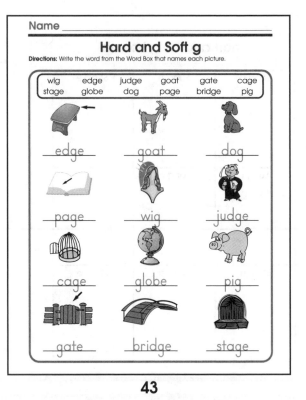

edge   goat   dog

page   wig   judge

cage   globe   pig

gate   bridge   stage

43

Name _____

Review: Hard and Soft c and g

Directions: Write the missing letter **c** or **g** for each word. Then, circle the word *hard* or *soft* to tell how the letter sounds.

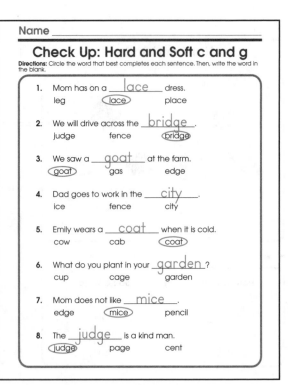

1. g as — (hard) soft
2. sta g e — hard (soft)
3. c age — (hard) soft
4. fa c e — hard (soft)
5. i c e — hard (soft)
6. brid g e — hard (soft)
7. c alf — (hard) soft
8. g arden — (hard) soft
9. jud g e — hard (soft)
10. mi c e — hard (soft)

44

Name _____

Check Up: Hard and Soft c and g

Directions: Circle the word that best completes each sentence. Then, write the word in the blank.

1. Mom has on a __lace__ dress.
   leg   (lace)   place
2. We will drive across the __bridge__.
   judge   fence   (bridge)
3. We saw a __goat__ at the farm.
   (goat)   gas   edge
4. Dad goes to work in the __city__.
   ice   fence   city
5. Emily wears a __coat__ when it is cold.
   cow   cab   (coat)
6. What do you plant in your __garden__?
   cup   cage   garden
7. Mom does not like __mice__.
   edge   (mice)   pencil
8. The __judge__ is a kind man.
   (judge)   page   cent

45

Answer Key

Name

Consonant Blends With S

Directions: Write the consonant blend that shows the beginning sound of each picture name.

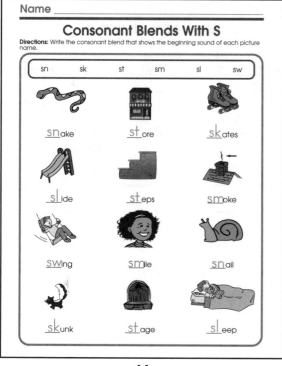

sn	sk	st	sm	sl	sw

snake store skates

slide steps smoke

swing smile snail

skunk stage sleep

46

Name

Consonant Blends With S

Directions: Write the word from the Word Box that names each picture.

square	snap	spoon	sled	store	scare

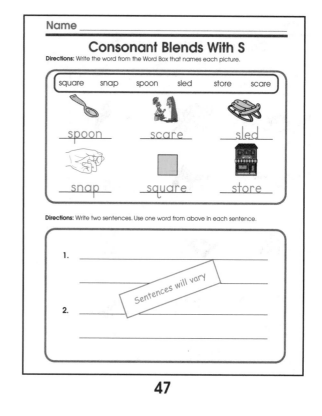

spoon scare sled

snap square store

Directions: Write two sentences. Use one word from above in each sentence.

1. _____

2. _____

Sentences will vary

47

Name

Consonant Blends With L

Directions: Write the consonant blend that shows the beginning sound of each picture name.

pl	cl	fl	gl	bl

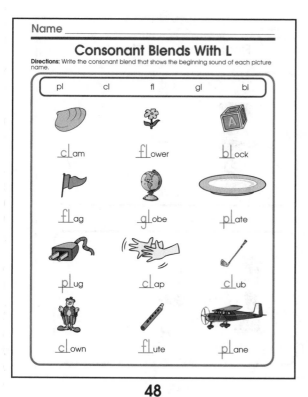

clam flower block

flag globe plate

plug clap club

clown flute plane

48

Name

Consonant Blends With L

Directions: Write the word from the Word Box that names each picture.

blow	clip	flame	glass	fly	flute

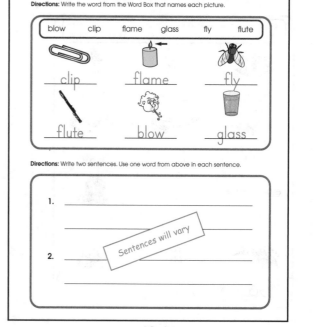

clip flame fly

flute blow glass

Directions: Write two sentences. Use one word from above in each sentence.

1. _____

2. _____

Sentences will vary

49

Answer Key

Name _____

Consonant Blends With R

Directions: Write the consonant blend that shows the beginning sound of each picture name.

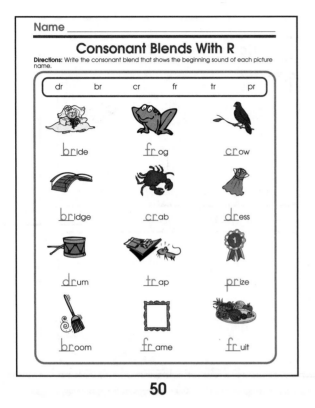

| dr | br | cr | fr | tr | pr |

bride   **fr**og   **cr**ow

bridge   **cr**ab   **dr**ess

drum   **tr**ap   **pr**ize

broom   **fr**ame   **fr**uit

50

Name _____

Consonant Blends With R

Directions: Write the word from the Word Box that names each picture.

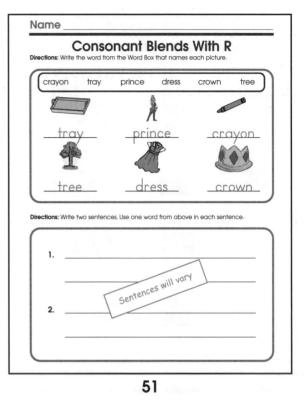

| crayon | tray | prince | dress | crown | tree |

tray   prince   crayon

tree   dress   crown

Directions: Write two sentences. Use one word from above in each sentence.

1. _____
   _____
   Sentences will vary
2. _____
   _____

51

Name _____

Review: Consonant Blends

Directions: Write the word from the Word Box that names each picture.

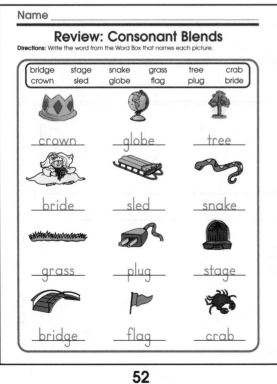

| bridge | stage | snake | grass | tree | crab |
| crown | sled | globe | flag | plug | bride |

crown   globe   tree

bride   sled   snake

grass   plug   stage

bridge   flag   crab

52

Name _____

Final Consonant Blends

Directions: Write the final consonant blend for each word. Then, write each word again.

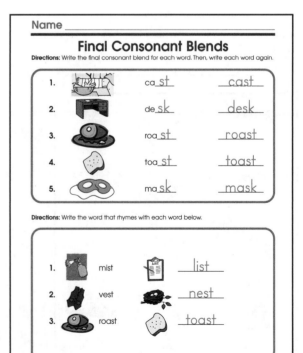

1. ca**st**   cast
2. de**sk**   desk
3. roa**st**   roast
4. toa**st**   toast
5. ma**sk**   mask

Directions: Write the word that rhymes with each word below.

1. mist   list
2. vest   nest
3. roast   toast

53

Answer Key

Name

Final Consonant Blends

Directions: Circle the consonant blend that you hear at the end of each picture name.

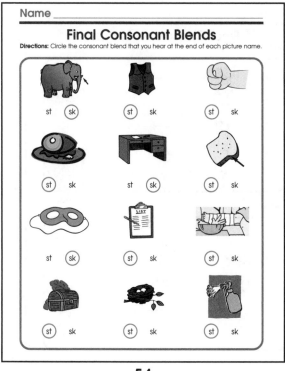

54

Name

Review: Final Consonant Blends

Directions: Write the word from the Word Box that names each picture.

mask	list	vest	desk	fist	mist
chest	tusk	roast	nest	crust	toast

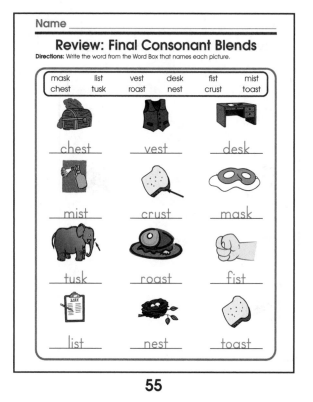

chest   vest   desk

mist   crust   mask

tusk   roast   fist

list   nest   toast

55

Name

Final Consonant Blends

Directions: Write the final consonant blend of each word. Then, write each word again.

1. sta**mp** stamp
2. pai **nt** paint
3. sku **nk** skunk
4. pla **nt** plant
5. ce **nt** cent

Directions: Write a word that rhymes with each word below.

1. band hand
2. stump pump
3. sink link

56

Name

Final Consonant Blends

Directions: Circle the word that names each picture.

(pond) point paint   bank (crank) cent

stand cent (tent)   pump (paint) plant

(lamp) pump stump   wink sink (wind)

band (bank) pond   (ant) stand and

stump (stamp) stand   stump pond (pump)

57

Spectrum Phonics Grade 2

141

Answer Key

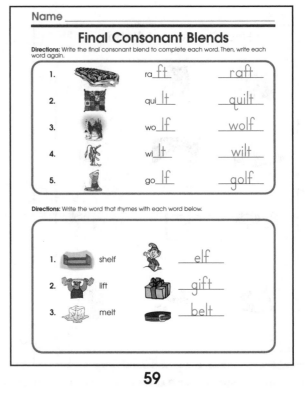

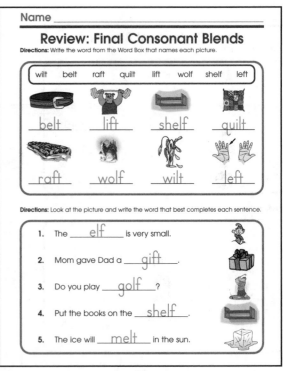

Answer Key

Three-Letter Consonant Blends

Directions: Write a three-letter consonant blend to complete each word. Then, write each word again.

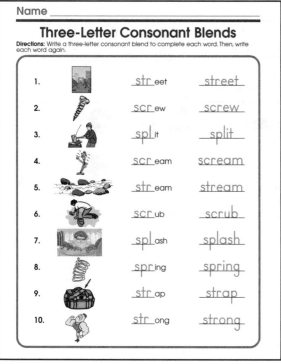

1. __str__ eet   street
2. __scr__ ew   screw
3. __spl__ it   split
4. __scr__ eam   scream
5. __str__ eam   stream
6. __scr__ ub   scrub
7. __spl__ ash   splash
8. __spr__ ing   spring
9. __str__ ap   strap
10. __str__ ong   strong

62

Three-Letter Consonant Blends

Directions: Draw a picture to go with each word below. Then, write a sentence that tells about each picture. Make sure to use the word in the sentence.

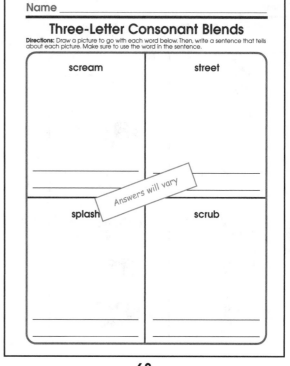

scream	street
splash	scrub

Answers will vary

63

Three-Letter Consonant Blends

Directions: Write the word from the Word Box that best completes each sentence.

stripes	scrape	street	sprain	scrub
spray	scrap	splash	stream	

1. There are many houses on my __street__ .
2. Dad will __spray__ the garden with the hose.
3. Steve makes a big __splash__ when he jumps in the pool.
4. Write your name on this __scrap__ of paper.
5. Grandpa and I fish in the __stream__ .
6. I do not like to __scrub__ the floor.
7. Oliver has a __scrape__ on his knee.
8. My new kitten has black and gray __stripes__ .
9. Mom got a bad __sprain__ when she fell.

64

Review: 3-Letter Consonant Blends

Directions: Write the word from the Word Box that names each picture.

scream	stripes	strap	street	strong	scrub
screw	spring	string	split	splash	stream

strap   stripes   splash

string   scream   stream

screw   street   split

scrub   strong   spring

65

Answer Key

Name _____

Check Up: Consonant Blends
Directions: Write a consonant blend to complete each word.

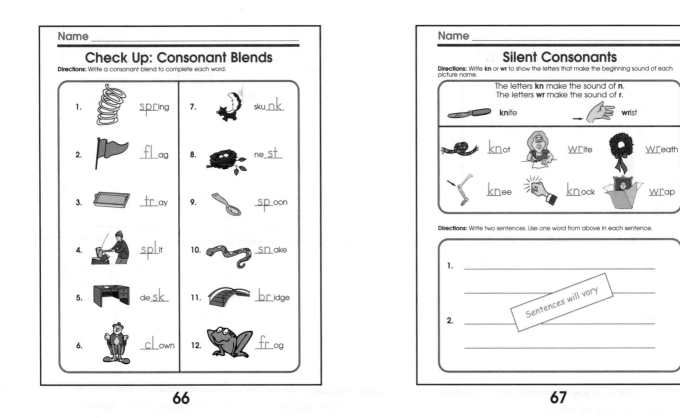

1. spr ing
2. fl ag
3. tr ay
4. spl it
5. de sk
6. cl own
7. sku nk
8. ne st
9. sp oon
10. sn ake
11. br idge
12. fr og

66

Name _____

Silent Consonants
Directions: Write **kn** or **wr** to show the letters that make the beginning sound of each picture name.

The letters **kn** make the sound of **n**.
The letters **wr** make the sound of **r**.

kn ife   wr ist

kn ot   wr ite   wr eath
kn ee   kn ock   wr ap

Directions: Write two sentences. Use one word from above in each sentence.

1. _____
2. _____

Sentences will vary

67

Name _____

Silent Consonants
Directions: Write the word from the Word Box that names each picture.

wrench	knock	wrist	kneel	write	knit

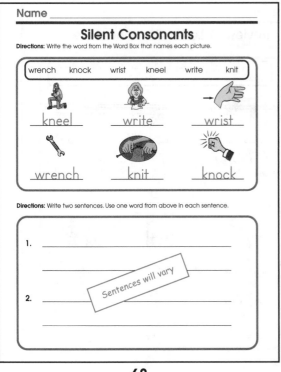

kneel   write   wrist
wrench   knit   knock

Directions: Write two sentences. Use one word from above in each sentence.

1. _____
2. _____

Sentences will vary

68

Name _____

Silent Consonants
Directions: Write the word from the Word Box that best completes each sentence.

knot	write	wrap	knife	wrong
know	knock	knee	knit	

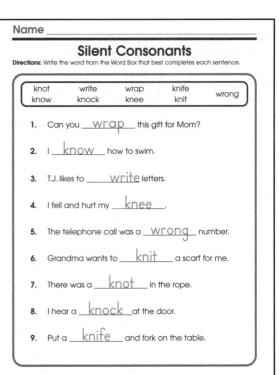

1. Can you __wrap__ this gift for Mom?
2. I __know__ how to swim.
3. T.J. likes to __write__ letters.
4. I fell and hurt my __knee__ .
5. The telephone call was a __wrong__ number.
6. Grandma wants to __knit__ a scarf for me.
7. There was a __knot__ in the rope.
8. I hear a __knock__ at the door.
9. Put a __knife__ and fork on the table.

69

Answer Key

Name _____

Silent Consonants

Directions: Write the word from the Word Box that names each picture.

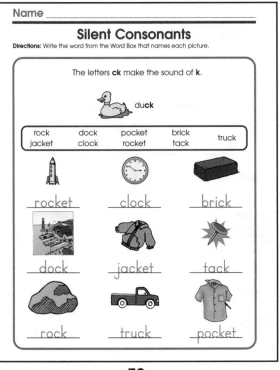

The letters **ck** make the sound of **k**.

duck

rock	dock	pocket	brick	
jacket	clock	rocket	tack	truck

rocket   clock   brick

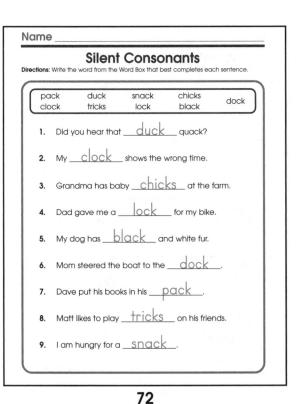

dock   jacket   tack

rock   truck   pocket

70

Name _____

Silent Consonants

Directions: Draw a picture to go with each word below. Then, write a sentence that tells about each picture. Make sure to use the word in the sentence.

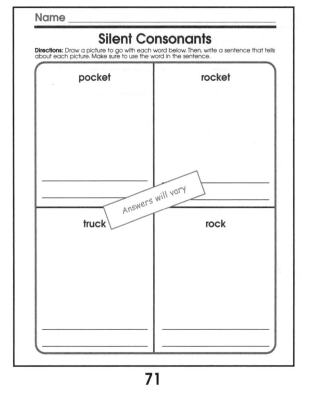

pocket	rocket
truck	rock

Answers will vary

71

Name _____

Silent Consonants

Directions: Write the word from the Word Box that best completes each sentence.

pack	duck	snack	chicks	
clock	tricks	lock	black	dock

1. Did you hear that __duck__ quack?

2. My __clock__ shows the wrong time.

3. Grandma has baby __chicks__ at the farm.

4. Dad gave me a __lock__ for my bike.

5. My dog has __black__ and white fur.

6. Mom steered the boat to the __dock__.

7. Dave put his books in his __pack__.

8. Matt likes to play __tricks__ on his friends.

9. I am hungry for a __snack__.

72

Name _____

Silent Consonants

Directions: Write the word from the Word Box that names each picture.

When **g** and **h** are together in a word, they are often silent.

 eight

eighty	light	knight	high	bright	night

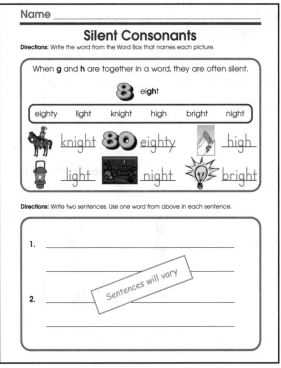

knight   eighty   high

light   night   bright

Directions: Write two sentences. Use one word from above in each sentence.

1. _____

2. _____

Sentences will vary

73

Answer Key

Silent Consonants

Directions: Write the word from the Word Box that best completes each sentence.

might	right	fight	night	sight
tight	eighty	light	high	

1. Grandpa is almost __eighty__ years old.

2. We __might__ not have school tomorrow.

3. My red jacket is too __tight__.

4. Mom was __right__ about the storm.

5. The snowy trees are a pretty __sight__.

6. The __light__ is very bright.

7. It rained all __night__ long.

8. I can't reach that __high__ shelf.

9. Dad doesn't like it when we __fight__.

74

Review: Silent Consonants

Directions: Write a sentence that tells about each picture.

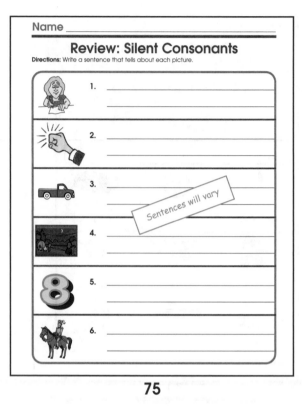

1. _____

2. _____

3. _____

Sentences will vary

4. _____

5. _____

6. _____

75

Check Up: Silent Consonants

Directions: Write the word from the Word Box that names each picture.

chicks	rock	lock	knit	knight	knock
wrist	write	pocket	wrap	knot	light

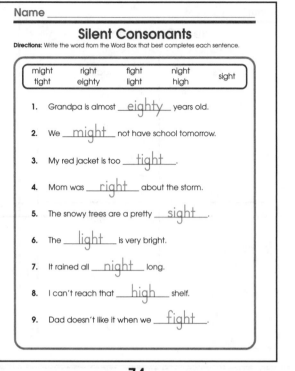

knight   rock   write

pocket   chicks   knot

knit   light   knock

wrist   wrap   lock

76

Vowel Pairs: AI and AY

Directions: The vowel pairs **ai** and **ay** can make the long **a** sound. Write the word that rhymes with each word below.

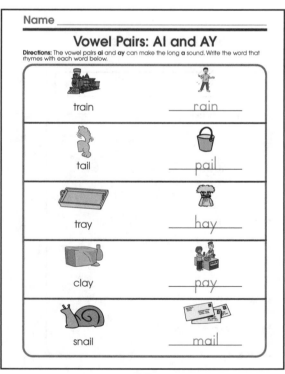

train	__rain__
tail	__pail__
tray	__hay__
clay	__pay__
snail	__mail__

77

Answer Key

Vowel Pairs: AI and AY

Directions: Write the word from the Word Box that names each picture.

clay	pail	tail	train	paint	mail
rain	stain	chain	pay	sail	tray

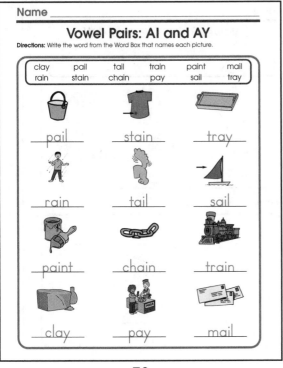

pail   stain   tray

rain   tail   sail

paint   chain   train

clay   pay   mail

78

Vowel Pairs: AI and AY

Directions: Write the word from the Word Box that best completes each sentence.

paint	tray	mail	snail	
rain	tail	clay	train	hay

1. The __snail__ is in its shell.

2. Dad brought us cookies on a __tray__.

3. The cows eat __hay__.

4. Kelly made a bowl from __clay__.

5. We don't like to play outside in the __rain__.

6. Fluffy wags his __tail__ when he is happy.

7. What color __paint__ should we use?

8. Grandma took the __train__ when she came to see us.

9. I bring in the __mail__ every day.

79

Vowel Pairs: EE and EA

Directions: The vowel pairs **ee** and **ea** can make the long **e** sound. Write the word from the Word Box that names each picture.

beads	tree	seal	bee	feet	seat

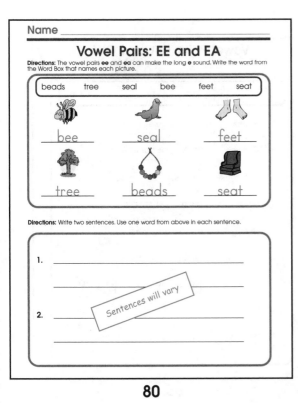

bee   seal   feet

tree   beads   seat

Directions: Write two sentences. Use one word from above in each sentence.

1. _____

2. _____

Sentences will vary

80

Vowel Pairs: EE and EA

Directions: Draw a picture to go with each word below. Then, write a sentence that tells about each picture. Make sure to use the word in the sentence.

leaf	beach
feet	sleep

Answers will vary

81

Answer Key

Name

Vowel Pairs: EE and EA

Directions: The vowel pair **ea** can also make the short **e** sound, as in *head*. Write the word from the Word Box that best completes each sentence.

bread	leak	steam	beak	sleep
beach	sheep	head	leap	

1. Our kitchen sink has a __leak__.

2. Do you like to swim at the __beach__?

3. The frog can __leap__ over the log.

4. Mom likes to bake wheat __bread__.

5. The bird has a very sharp __beak__.

6. A baby __sheep__ is called a lamb.

7. James hit his __head__ on the shelf.

8. Ryan and Eric will __sleep__ in the tent tonight.

9. I see __steam__ coming from the teakettle.

82

Name

Vowel Pairs: OA and OW

Directions: The vowel pairs **oa** and **ow** can make the long **o** sound. Write the word from the Word Box that names each picture.

pillow	goat	snow	road	crow	soap

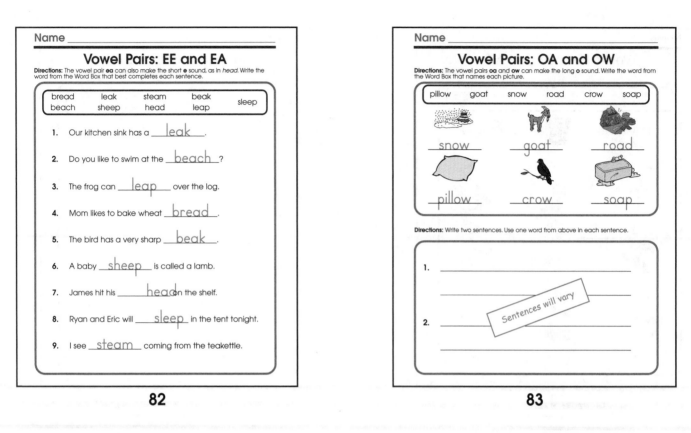

__snow__ __goat__ __road__

__pillow__ __crow__ __soap__

Directions: Write two sentences. Use one word from above in each sentence.

1. _____

2. _____

Sentences will vary

83

Name

Vowel Pairs: OA and OW

Directions: Draw a picture to go with each word below. Then, write a sentence that tells about each picture. Make sure to use the word in the sentence.

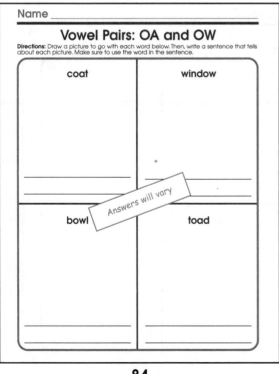

coat	window
bowl	toad

Answers will vary

84

Name

Vowel Pairs: OA and OW

Directions: Write the word from the Word Box that best completes each sentence.

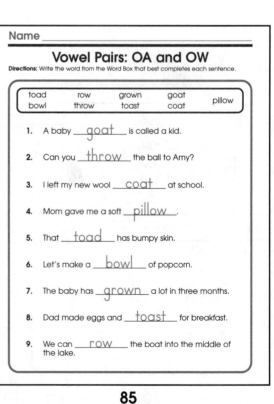

toad	row	grown	goat	pillow
bowl	throw	toast	coat	

1. A baby __goat__ is called a kid.

2. Can you __throw__ the ball to Amy?

3. I left my new wool __coat__ at school.

4. Mom gave me a soft __pillow__.

5. That __toad__ has bumpy skin.

6. Let's make a __bowl__ of popcorn.

7. The baby has __grown__ a lot in three months.

8. Dad made eggs and __toast__ for breakfast.

9. We can __row__ the boat into the middle of the lake.

85

Answer Key

Name _____

Review: Vowel Pairs

Directions: Write the missing vowel pair for each word. Then, write each word again.

1. b_ea_k beak
2. h_ay hay
3. s_oa_p soap
4. br_ea_d bread
5. sl_ee_p sleep
6. b_ow_l bowl
7. s_ea_l seal
8. sn_ai_l snail
9. l_ea_f leaf
10. cr_ow crow

86

Name _____

Vowel Pair: OO

Directions: The vowel pair **oo** can make a short sound, as in *hook,* and a long sound, as in *moon.* Write the word that rhymes with each word below.

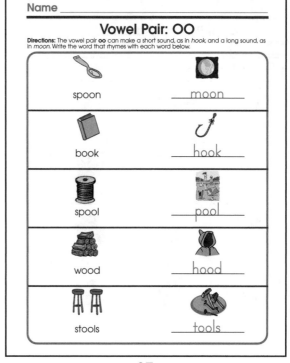

spoon — moon

book — hook

spool — pool

wood — hood

stools — tools

87

Name _____

Vowel Pair: OO

Directions: Write the word from the Word Box that names each picture.

| spoon | boot | moose | hoop | moon | pool |
| woods | tooth | hood | hoof | broom | book |

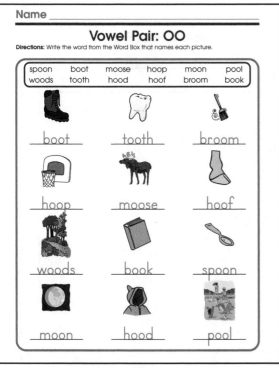

boot   tooth   broom

hoop   moose   hoof

woods   book   spoon

moon   hood   pool

88

Name _____

Vowel Pairs: AU and AW

Directions: The vowel pairs **au** and **aw** can make the sound that you hear in the middle of the words *cause* and *lawn.* In each row, write the two words that rhyme with the first word in the row.

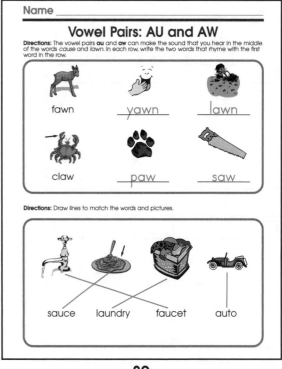

fawn   yawn   lawn

claw   paw   saw

Directions: Draw lines to match the words and pictures.

sauce   laundry   faucet   auto

89

Answer Key

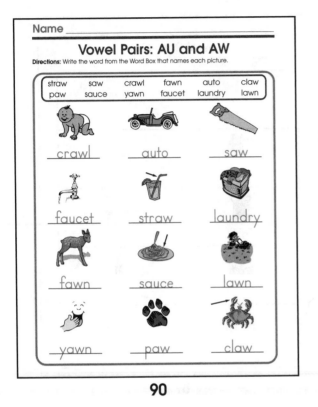

Vowel Pairs: AU and AW

Directions: Write the word from the Word Box that names each picture.

| straw | saw | crawl | fawn | auto | claw |
| paw | sauce | yawn | faucet | laundry | lawn |

crawl auto saw

faucet straw laundry

fawn sauce lawn

yawn paw claw

90

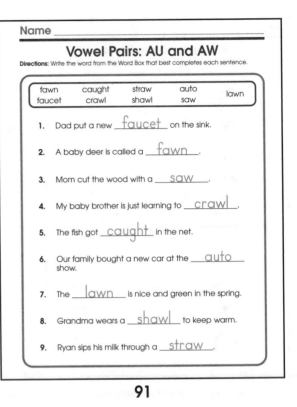

Vowel Pairs: AU and AW

Directions: Write the word from the Word Box that best completes each sentence.

| fawn | caught | straw | auto | |
| faucet | crawl | shawl | saw | lawn |

1. Dad put a new __faucet__ on the sink.

2. A baby deer is called a __fawn__.

3. Mom cut the wood with a __saw__.

4. My baby brother is just learning to __crawl__.

5. The fish got __caught__ in the net.

6. Our family bought a new car at the __auto__ show.

7. The __lawn__ is nice and green in the spring.

8. Grandma wears a __shawl__ to keep warm.

9. Ryan sips his milk through a __straw__.

91

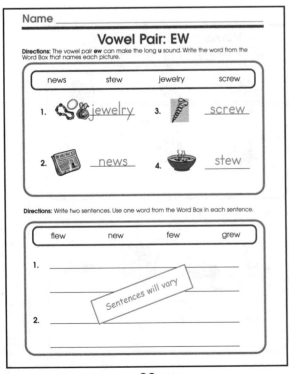

Vowel Pair: EW

Directions: The vowel pair **ew** can make the long **u** sound. Write the word from the Word Box that names each picture.

| news | stew | jewelry | screw |

1. __jewelry__   3. __screw__

2. __news__   4. __stew__

Directions: Write two sentences. Use one word from the Word Box in each sentence.

| flew | new | few | grew |

1. _____

2. _____

Sentences will vary

92

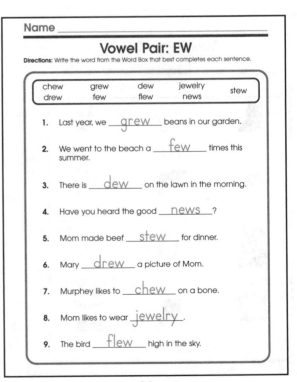

Vowel Pair: EW

Directions: Write the word from the Word Box that best completes each sentence.

| chew | grew | dew | jewelry | |
| drew | few | flew | news | stew |

1. Last year, we __grew__ beans in our garden.

2. We went to the beach a __few__ times this summer.

3. There is __dew__ on the lawn in the morning.

4. Have you heard the good __news__?

5. Mom made beef __stew__ for dinner.

6. Mary __drew__ a picture of Mom.

7. Murphey likes to __chew__ on a bone.

8. Mom likes to wear __jewelry__.

9. The bird __flew__ high in the sky.

93

Answer Key

Review: Vowel Pairs

Directions: Write the word from the Word Box that names each picture.

auto	yawn	stew	hood	faucet	fawn
laundry	screw	tooth	claw	book	moose

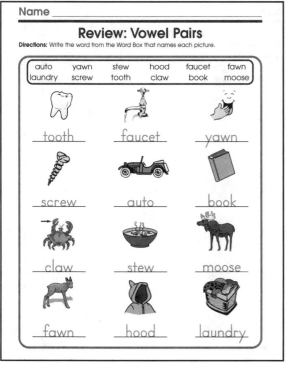

tooth   faucet   yawn

screw   auto   book

claw   stew   moose

fawn   hood   laundry

94

The Sounds of Y

Directions: Read the words. Write each word in the correct column.

Sometimes **y** can sound like long **e**, and sometimes it can sound like long **i**.

puppy   fry

dry   baby   city   sky

pony   fly   bunny   cry

Y as Long e	Y as Long i
pony	dry
baby	sky
city	fly
bunny	cry

95

The Sounds of Y

Directions: Write the word from the Word Box that names each picture.

bunny	fly	cry	money	muddy	city
puppy	sky	baby	fry	key	dry

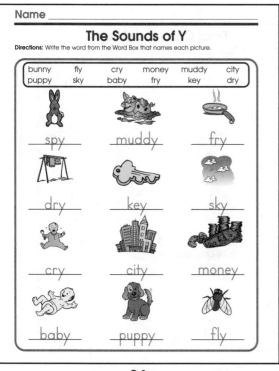

spy   muddy   fry

dry   key   sky

cry   city   money

baby   puppy   fly

96

The Sounds of Y

Directions: Write the word from the Word Box that best completes each sentence.

silly	cry	city	story	
try	muddy	happy	fry	puppy

1. Can you hear the baby ___cry___?

2. The ___city___ is a busy place.

3. Dad will ___try___ not to be late.

4. It is ___muddy___ after it rains.

5. My brother takes good care of his new ___puppy___.

6. Elise is ___happy___ when she reads.

7. Molly will read us a ___story___.

8. Josh told us a ___silly___ joke.

9. Do you know how to ___fry___ an egg?

97

Answer Key

Name _____

Check Up: Vowel Pairs and Sounds of Y

Directions: Write the name of each picture.

fly   boot   train

bread   coat   leaf

bowl   feet   book

saw   baby   hay

screw   sauce   broom

98

Name _____

Consonant Pairs

Directions: Write the letters **sh**, **ch**, **th**, or **wh** to complete each word. Then, write each word again.

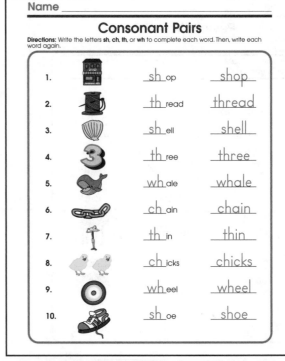

1. __sh__ op   shop
2. __th__ read   thread
3. __sh__ ell   shell
4. __th__ ree   three
5. __wh__ ale   whale
6. __ch__ ain   chain
7. __th__ in   thin
8. __ch__ icks   chicks
9. __wh__ eel   wheel
10. __sh__ oe   shoe

99

Name _____

Consonant Pairs

Directions: Write the word from the Word Box that names each picture.

wheel	ship	chair	whale	shoe	shelf
think	cheese	throat	thread	cheek	thin

throat   think   ship

wheel   shoe   thin

whale   shelf   cheese

thread   chair   cheek

100

Name _____

Final Consonant Pairs

Directions: Write the final consonant pair **sh**, **ch**, **tch**, **th**, or **ng** to complete each word. Then, write each word again.

1. ri__ng__   ring
2. spr__ing__   spring
3. di__sh__   dish
4. bran__ch__   branch
5. chur__ch__   church
6. stri__ng__   string
7. ba__th__   bath
8. bru__sh__   brush
9. wi__ng__   wing
10. too__th__   tooth

101

Answer Key

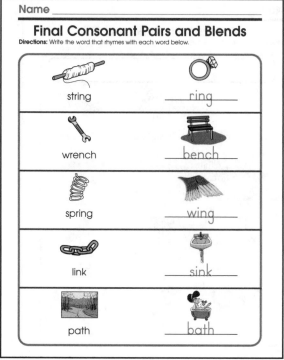
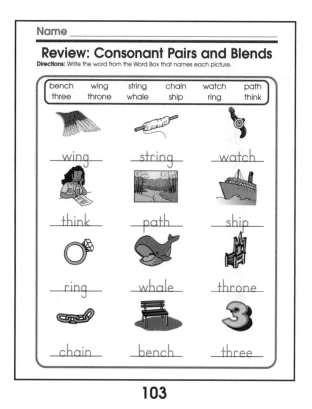
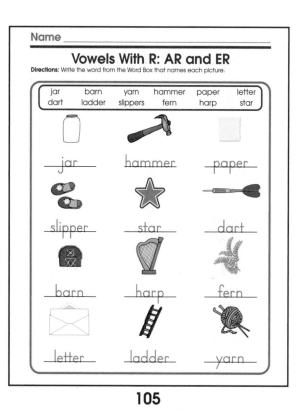

Answer Key

Vowels With R: AR and ER

Directions: Write the missing letters **ar** or **er** for each word. Then, write each word again.

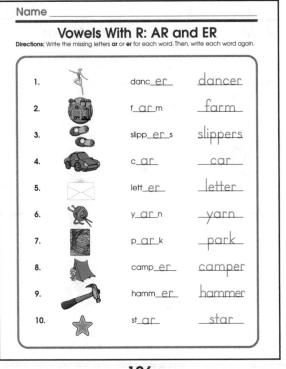

1. danc_er_   dancer
2. f_ar_m   farm
3. slipp_er_s   slippers
4. c_ar_   car
5. lett_er_   letter
6. y_ar_n   yarn
7. p_ar_k   park
8. camp_er_   camper
9. hamm_er_   hammer
10. st_ar_   star

106

Vowels With R: IR and OR

Directions: Write the word from the Word Box that names each picture.

| dirt | thorn | bird | girl | corn | fort |
| storm | cork | thirty | fork | shirt | skirt |

cork   girl   corn

dirt   fork   storm

skirt   shirt   bird

thirty   thorn   fort

107

Vowels With R: IR and OR

Directions: Write the missing letters **ir** or **or** for each word. Then, write each word again.

1. h_or_se   horse
2. sk_ir_t   skirt
3. f_or_k   fork
4. st_or_m   storm
5. g_ir_l   girl
6. c_or_n   corn
7. sh_ir_t   shirt
8. b_ir_d   bird
9. th_or_n   thorn
10. c_or_d   cord

108

Vowels With R: UR

Directions: Write the word from the Word Box that names each picture.

| hurt | fur | turn | burn | curb |

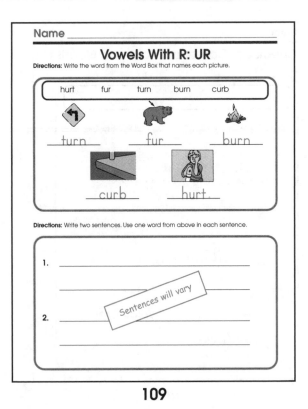

turn   fur   burn

curb   hurt

Directions: Write two sentences. Use one word from above in each sentence.

1. _____
   _____
   Sentences will vary
2. _____
   _____

109

Spectrum Phonics Grade 2

Answer Key

Name _____

Vowels With R
Directions: Write the word that rhymes with each word below.

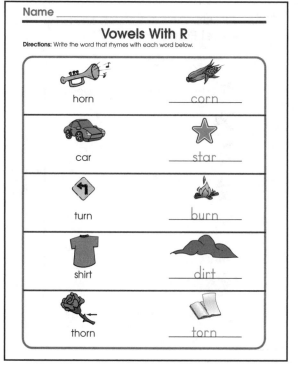

horn	corn
car	star
turn	burn
shirt	dirt
thorn	torn

110

Name _____

Vowels With R
Directions: Write the word from the Word Box that best completes each sentence.

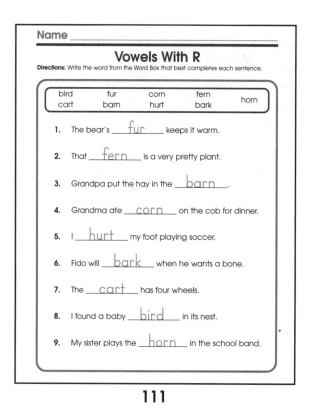

bird	fur	corn	fern	
cart	barn	hurt	bark	horn

1. The bear's __fur__ keeps it warm.

2. That __fern__ is a very pretty plant.

3. Grandpa put the hay in the __barn__.

4. Grandma ate __corn__ on the cob for dinner.

5. I __hurt__ my foot playing soccer.

6. Fido will __bark__ when he wants a bone.

7. The __cart__ has four wheels.

8. I found a baby __bird__ in its nest.

9. My sister plays the __horn__ in the school band.

111

Name _____

Review: Vowels With R
Directions: Write the word from the Word Box that names each picture.

fork	shirt	hurt	bird	star	burn
letter	turn	fern	horn	car	barn

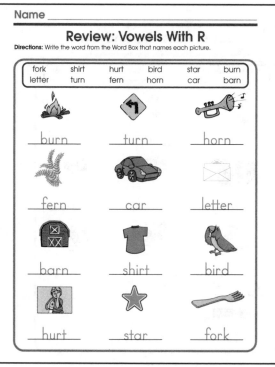

burn	turn	horn
fern	car	letter
barn	shirt	bird
hurt	star	fork

112

Name _____

Check Up: Vowels With R
Directions: Write six sentences. Use one word from the Word Box in each sentence.

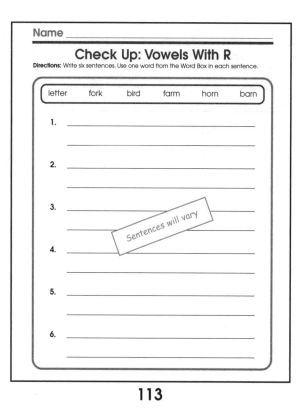

letter	fork	bird	farm	horn	barn

1. _____

2. _____

3. _____

Sentences will vary

4. _____

5. _____

6. _____

113

Answer Key

Name _____
Vowel Pairs: OI and OY
Directions: The vowel pairs **oi** and **oy** can make the sound that you hear in the middle of the words *noise* and *boys*. Write the word from the Word Box that names each picture.

boil	boys	soil	coins	point	toys

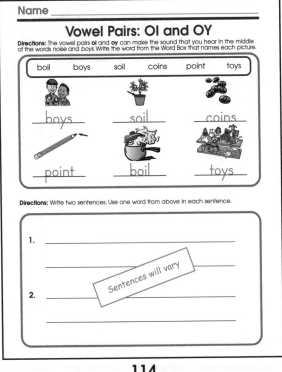

boys   soil   coins

point   boil   toys

Directions: Write two sentences. Use one word from above in each sentence.

1. _____

_____

Sentences will vary

2. _____

_____

114

Name _____
Vowel Pairs: OI and OY
Directions: Write the missing letters **oi** or **oy** for each word. Then, write the word again.

1. b_oi_l   boil
2. c_oi_ns   coins
3. b_oy_s   boys
4. s_oi_l   soil
5. _oy_ster   oyster
6. _oi_l   oil
7. t_oy_s   toys
8. p_oi_nt   point

115

Name _____
Vowel Pairs: OI and OY
Directions: Write the word from the Word Box that best completes each sentence.

boys	voice	enjoys	noise	
soil	join	toys	coins	point

1. Her loud __voice__ hurts my ears.
2. I broke the __point__ on my pencil.
3. How many __coins__ do you have in your pocket?
4. We gave the baby two new __toys__ to play with.
5. Our car is making a funny __noise__.
6. Those __boys__ are friends from school.
7. Mark is going to __join__ the reading club.
8. We got the __soil__ ready so we could plant our garden.
9. Mom __enjoys__ going to the library.

116

Name _____
Vowel Pairs: OU and OW
Directions: The vowel pairs **ou** and **ow** can make the sound you hear in the middle of *mouth* and *clown*. Write the word from the Word Box that names each picture.

shower	pound	plow	crown	house	clown
cow	blouse	flower	bounce	frown	gown

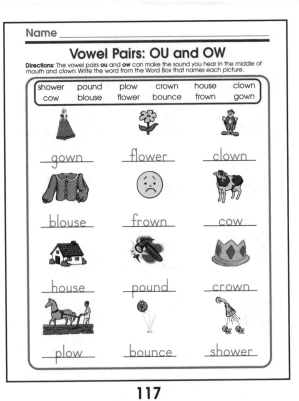

gown   flower   clown

blouse   frown   cow

house   pound   crown

plow   bounce   shower

117

Spectrum Phonics Grade 2

156

Answer Key

Name _____

Vowel Pairs: OU and OW

Directions: Write the missing letters **ou** or **ow** for each word. Then, write each word again.

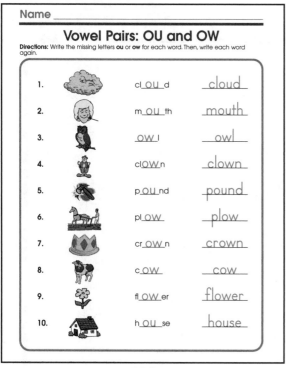

1.		cl_ou_d	cloud
2.		m_ou_th	mouth
3.		_ow_l	owl
4.		cl_ow_n	clown
5.		p_ou_nd	pound
6.		pl_ow_	plow
7.		cr_ow_n	crown
8.		c_ow_	cow
9.		fl_ow_er	flower
10.		h_ou_se	house

118

Name _____

Vowel Pairs: OU and OW

Directions: Write the word from the Word Box that best completes each sentence.

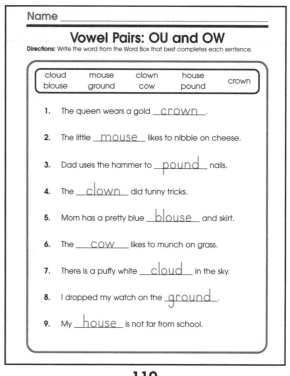

cloud	mouse	clown	house	crown
blouse	ground	cow	pound	

1. The queen wears a gold __crown__ .

2. The little __mouse__ likes to nibble on cheese.

3. Dad uses the hammer to __pound__ nails.

4. The __clown__ did funny tricks.

5. Mom has a pretty blue __blouse__ and skirt.

6. The __cow__ likes to munch on grass.

7. There is a puffy white __cloud__ in the sky.

8. I dropped my watch on the __ground__ .

9. My __house__ is not far from school.

119

Name _____

Review: Vowel Pairs

Directions: Write the word that rhymes with each word below.

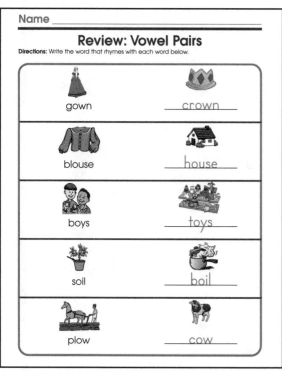

gown	crown
blouse	house
boys	toys
soil	boil
plow	cow

120

Name _____

Check Up: Vowel Pairs

Directions: Write a word that names each picture. Each word should have the **oi, oy, ou,** or **ow** vowel pair.

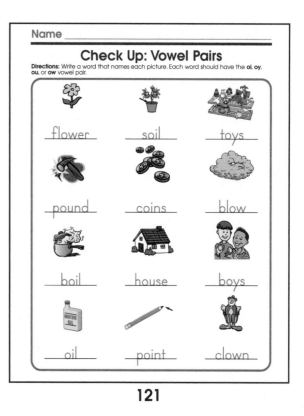

flower	soil	toys
pound	coins	blow
boil	house	boys
oil	point	clown

121

Notes

Notes

Notes